The first photo in this book repeats dozens of times as source for the uniqueness of every page. A good close look at each variation of the original photo will eventually yield this truth, but readers are encouraged to seek the balance and structure of each version as they individually vary rather than attempting to find that which they hold in common. As with my Artists of Big Sur volume, this book deals with computational post-processing using a variety of off-the-shclf apps and personal algorithms that provide the contrasting variations.

The Bells
Of
St. Mary's

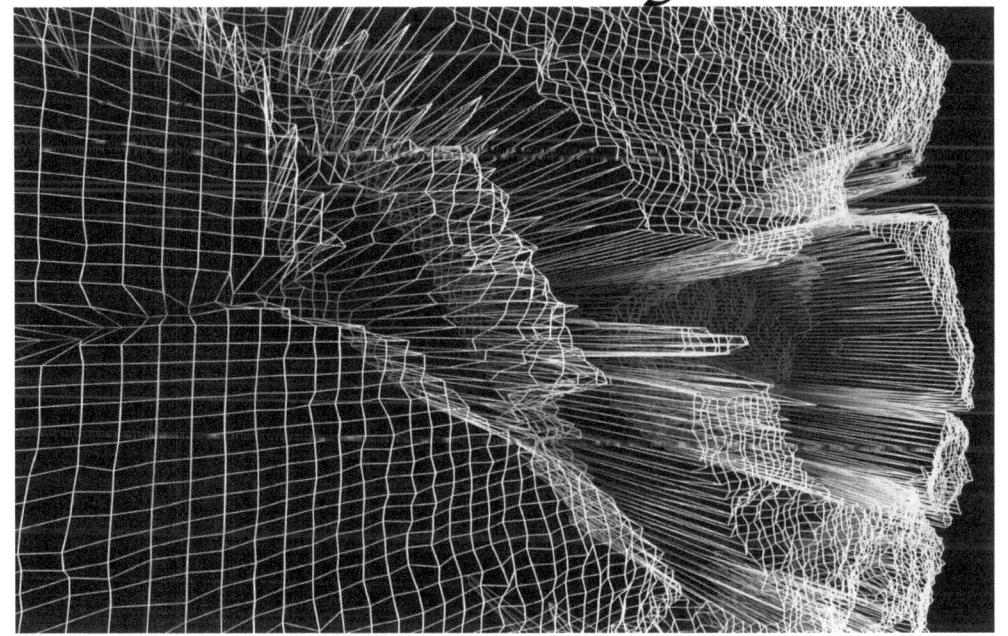

Photographs
By
David Cope

The Bells of Saint Mary's
Photographs by David Cope

Epoc Books
Printed in the United States of America
© David Cope 2016
All Rights Reserved.
Published 2016.

This book is dedicated to my wife, sons, and grandchildren, Zoe, Tess, Gavin, and Ethan whose excitement for everyday things never ceases to amaze me. And to those older kids like me who believe in those children.

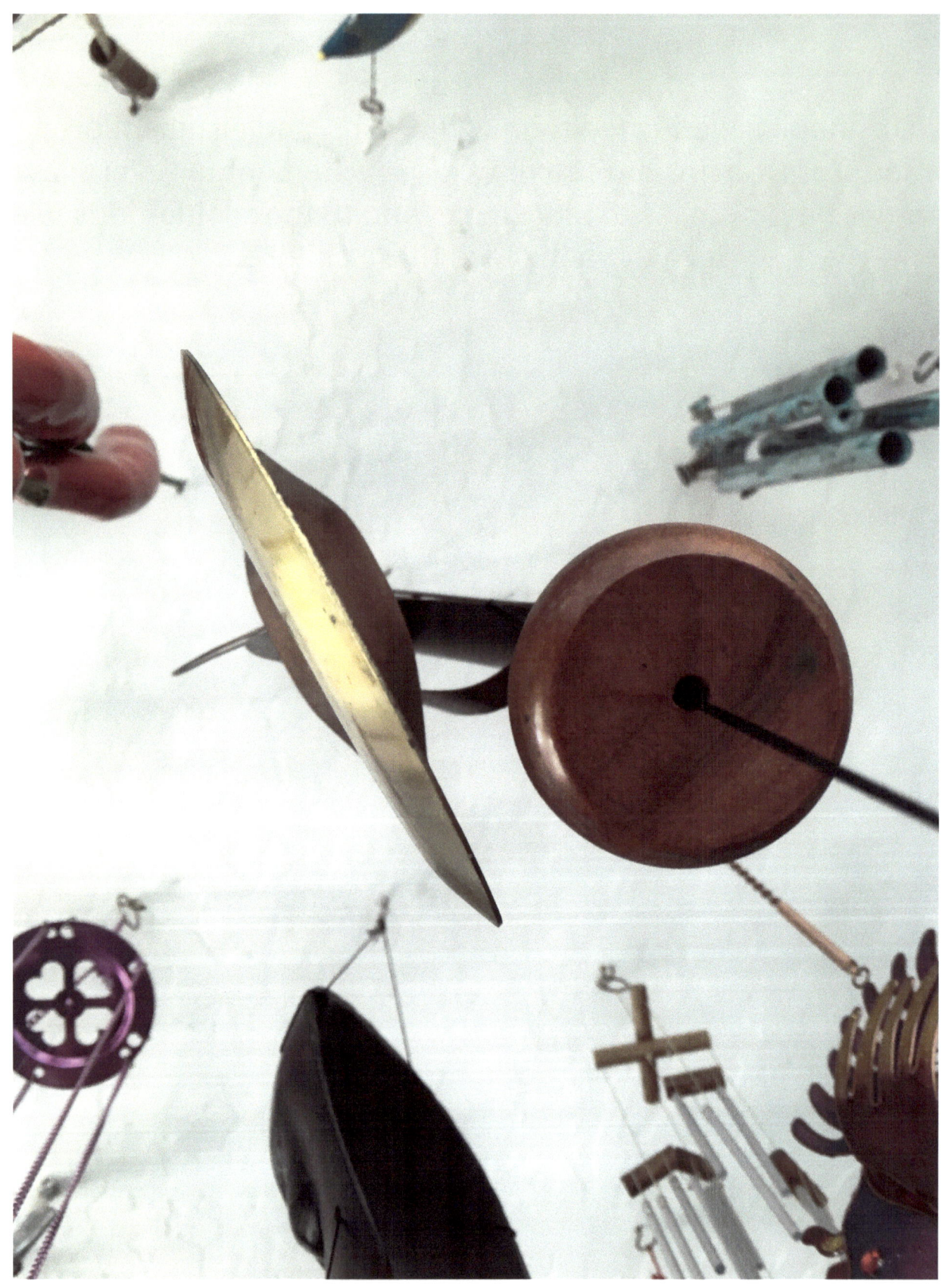

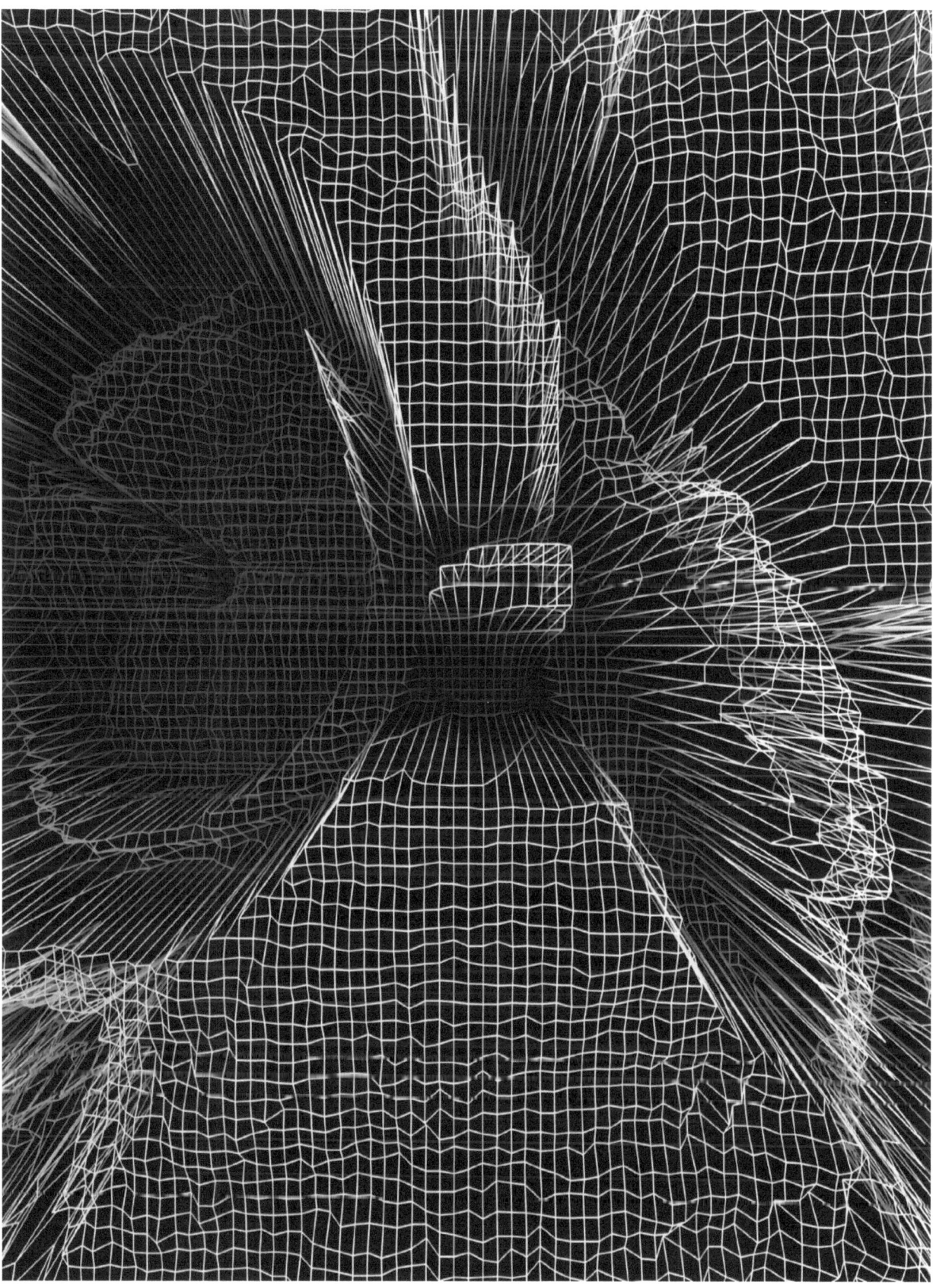

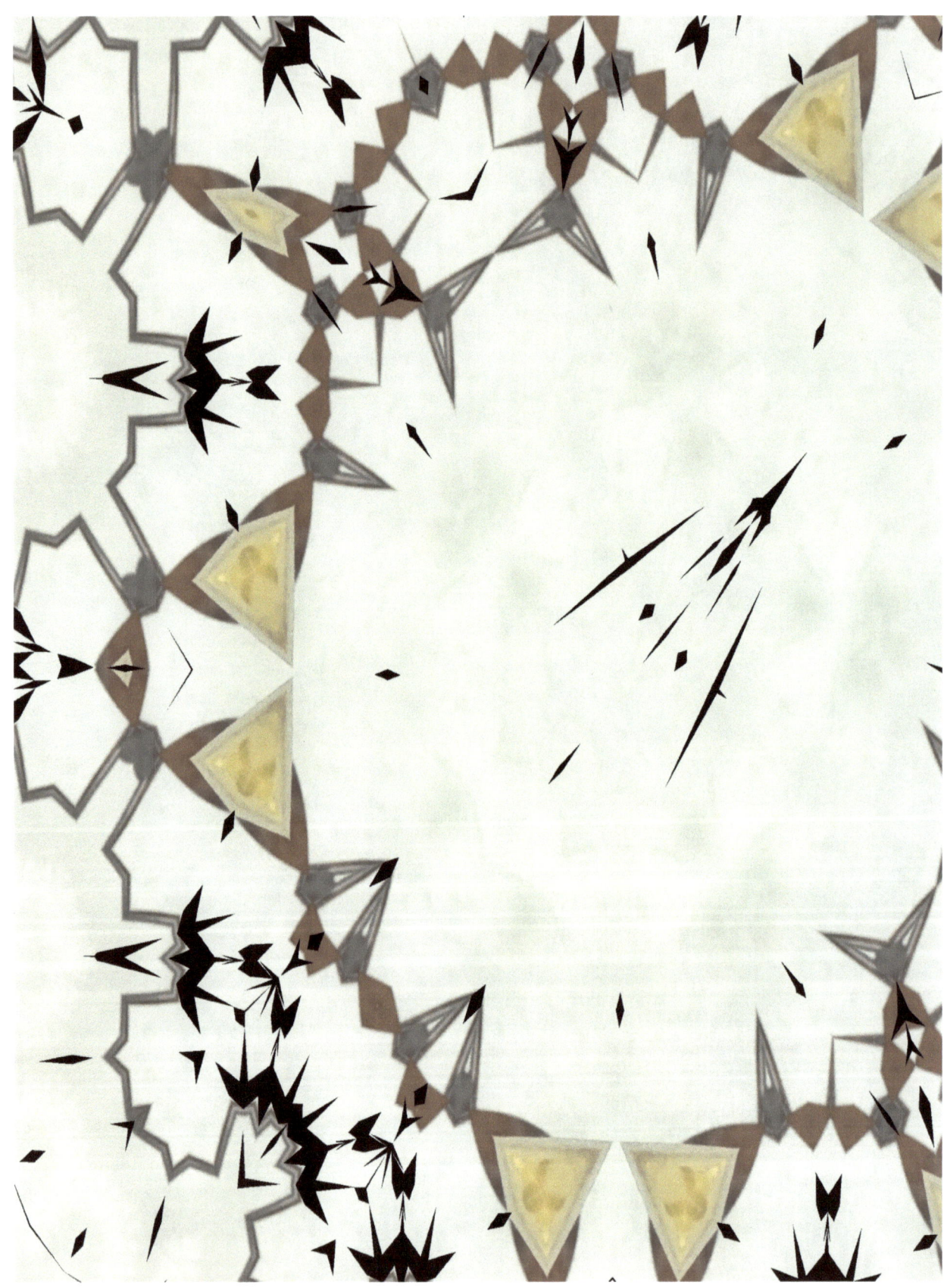

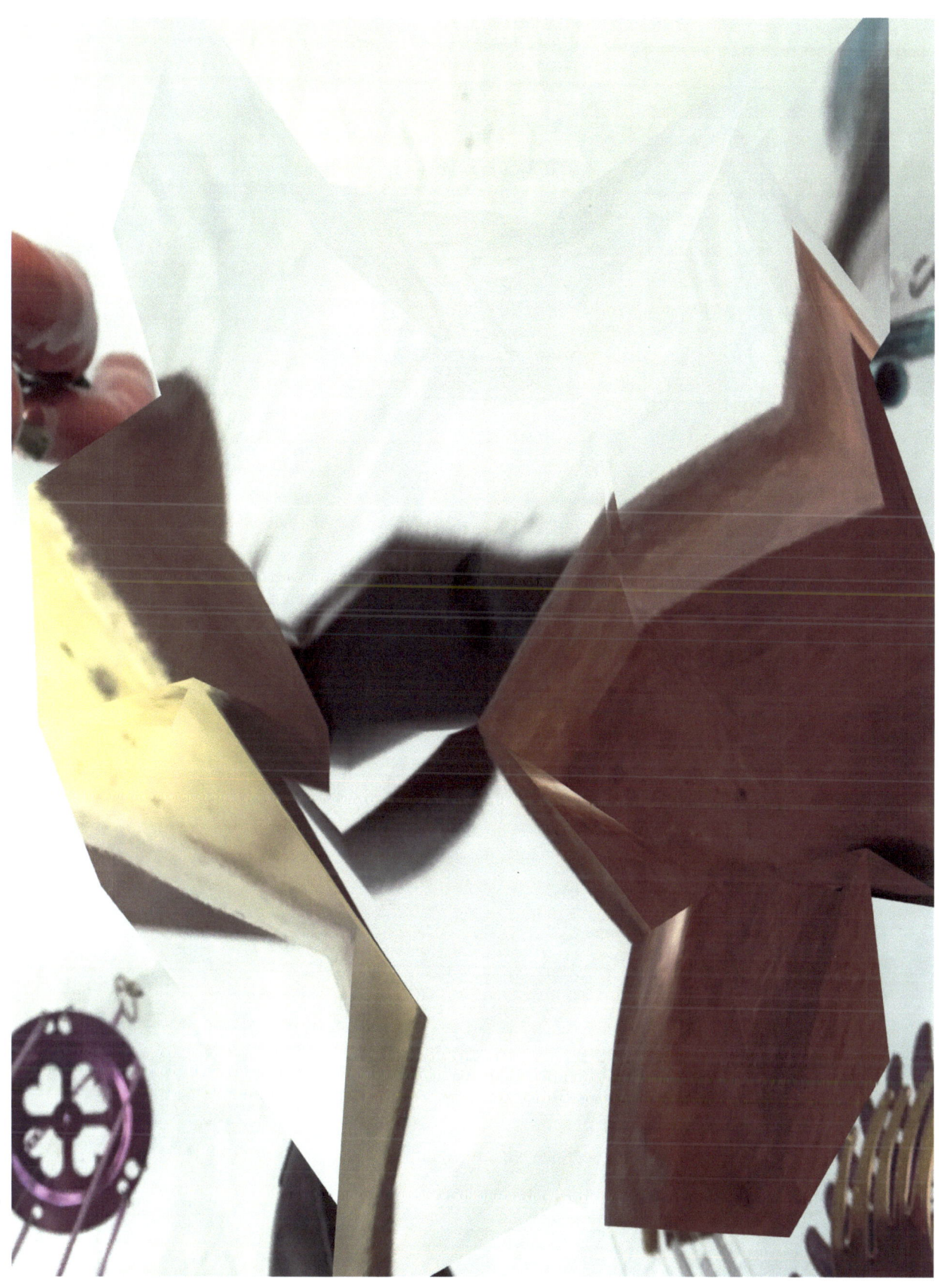

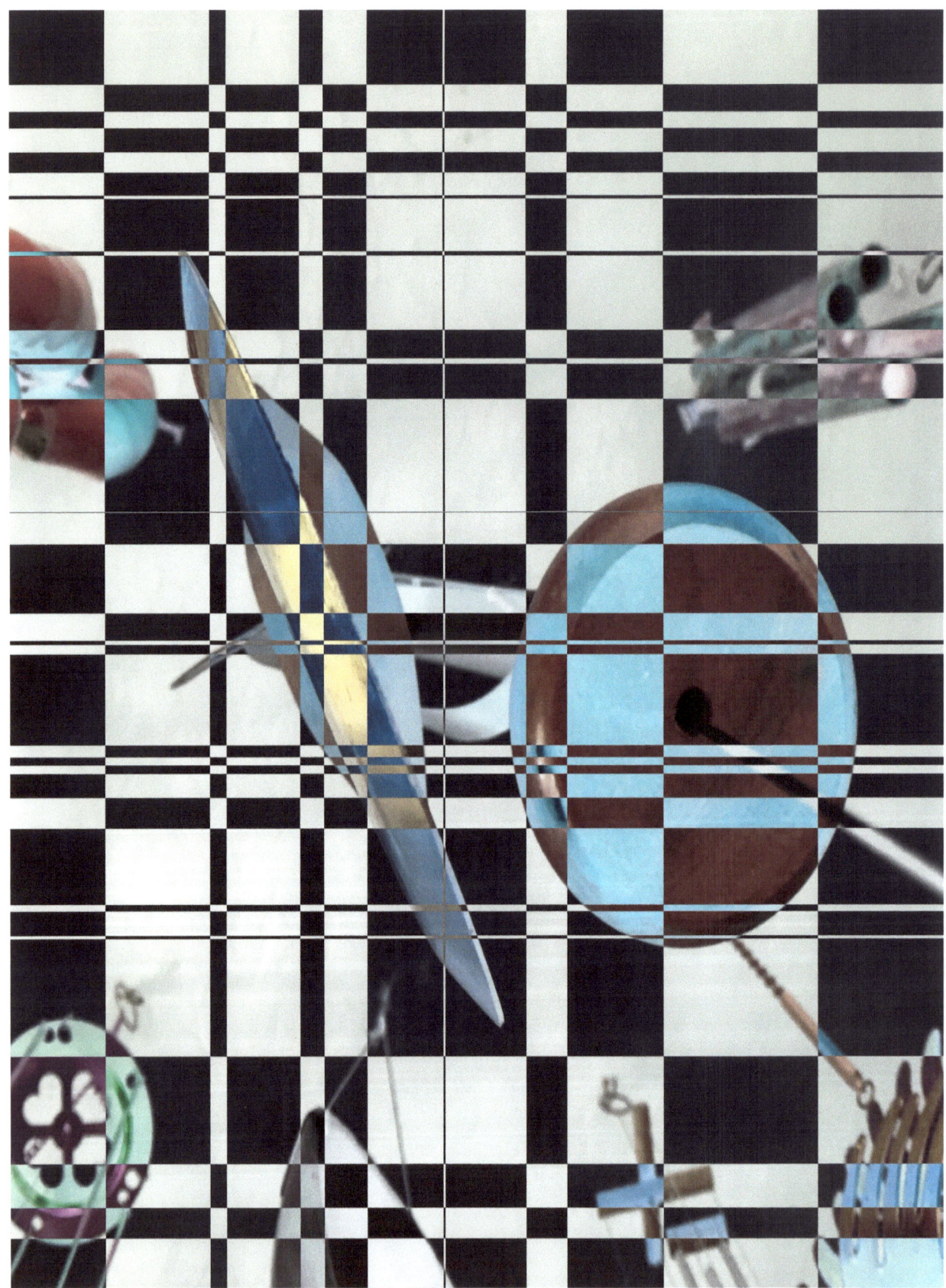

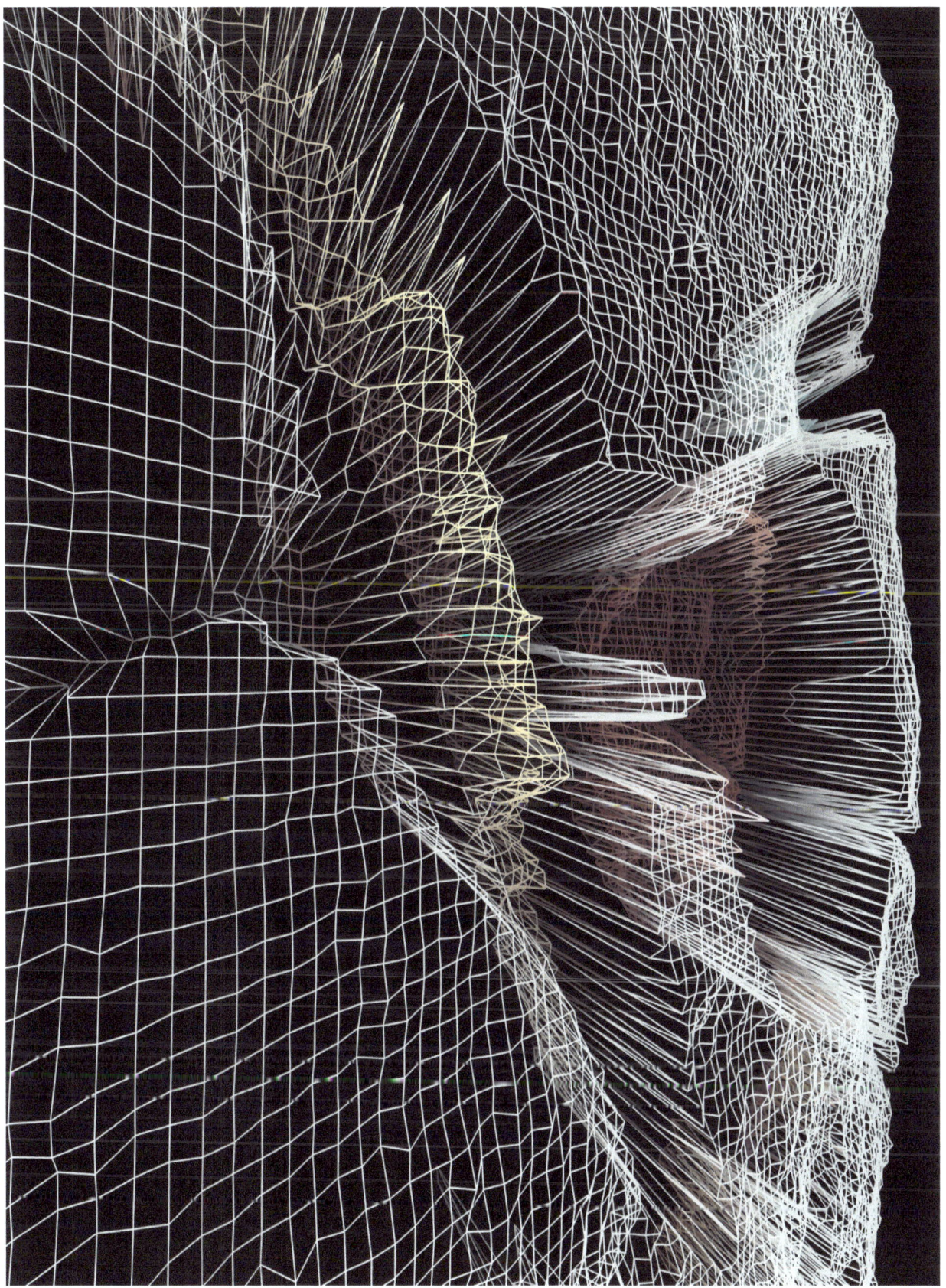

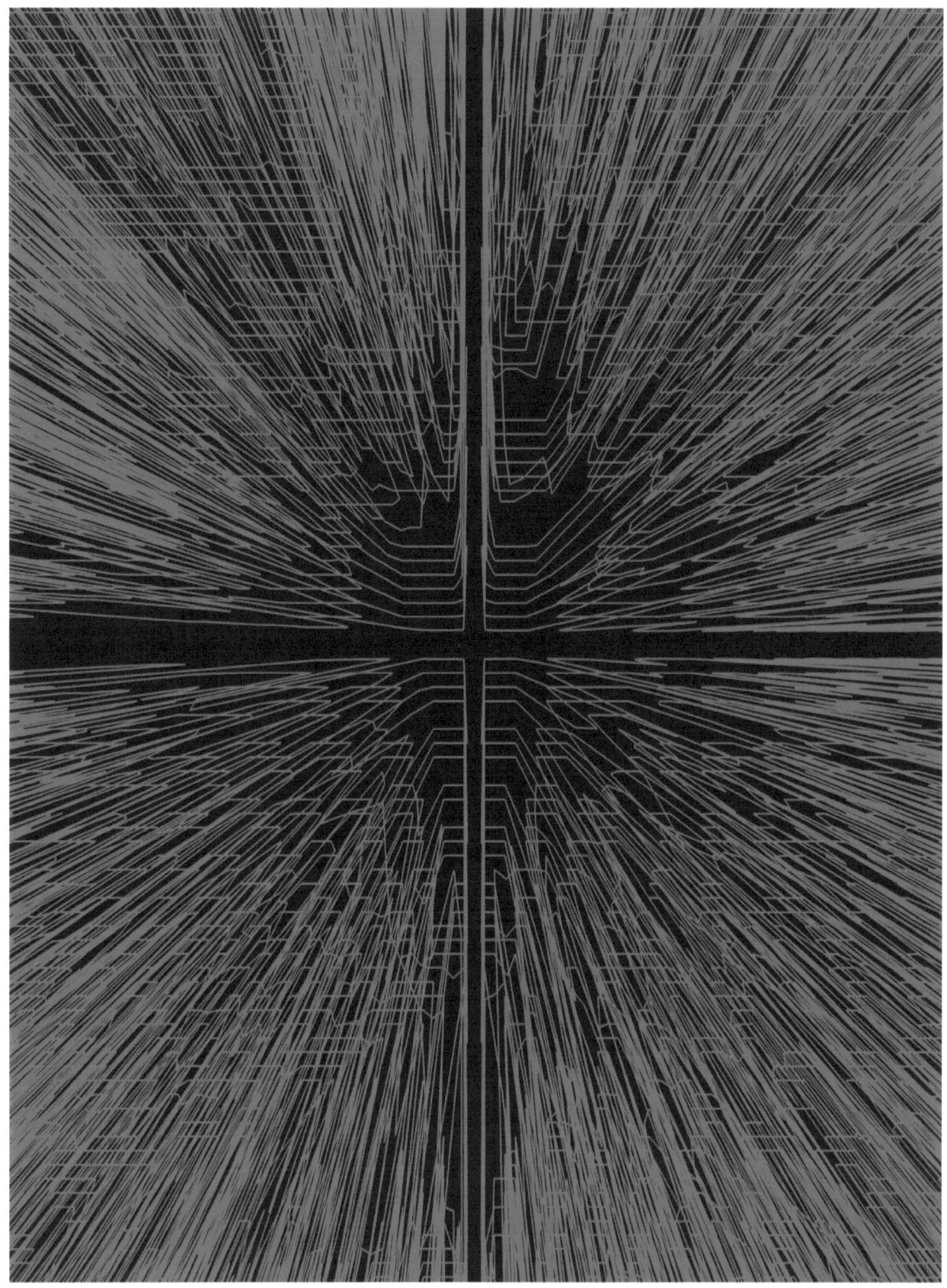

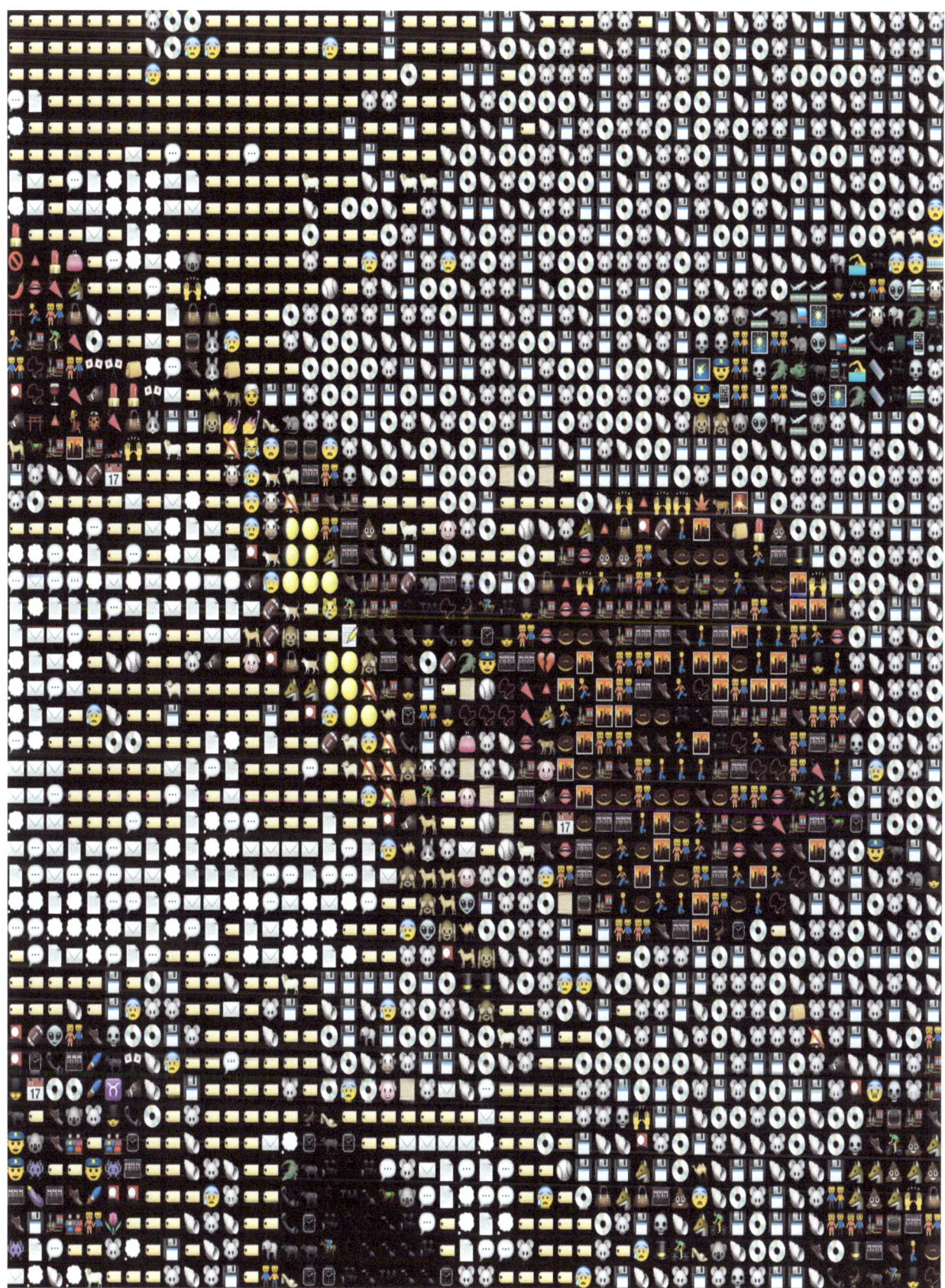

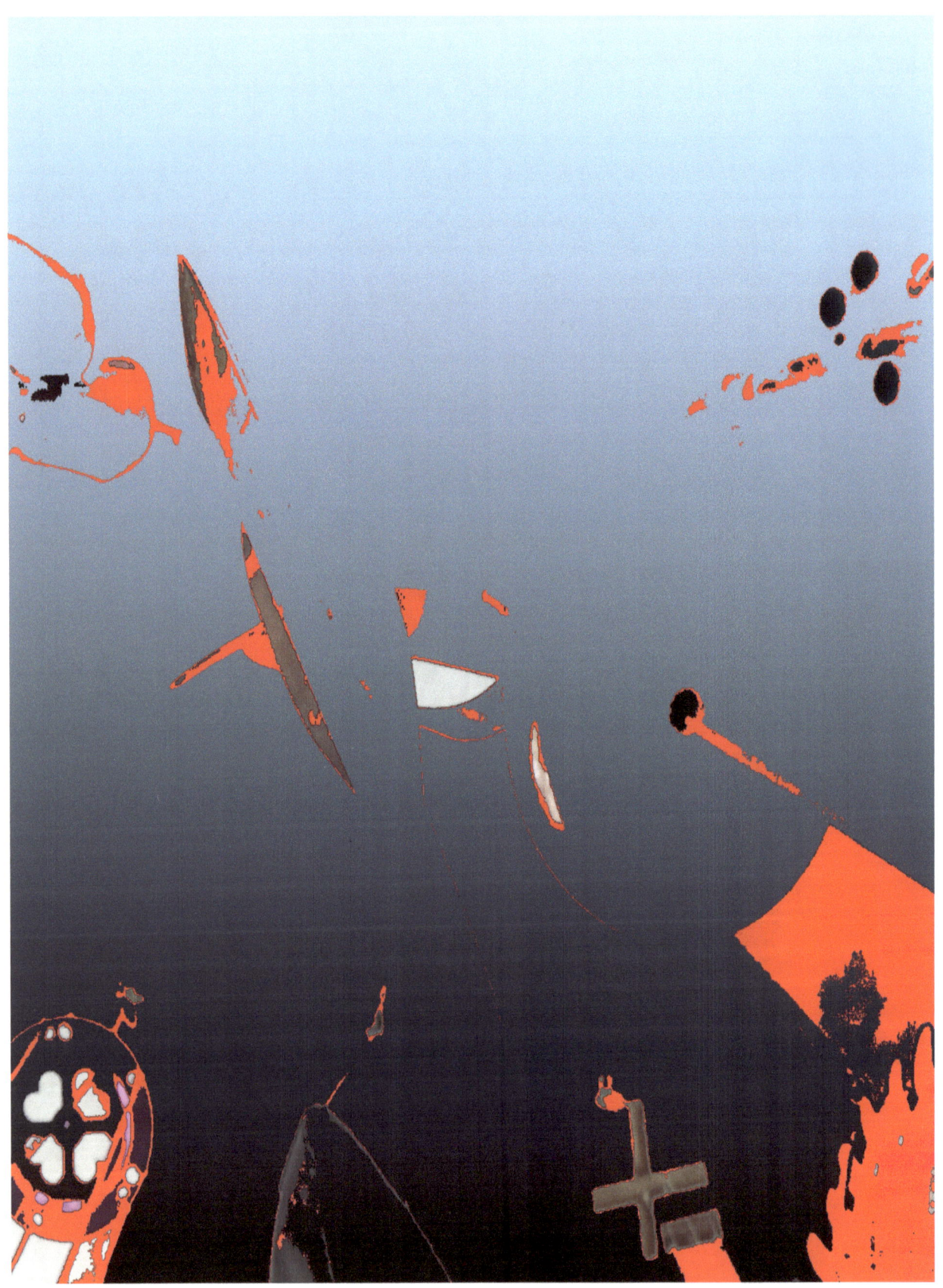

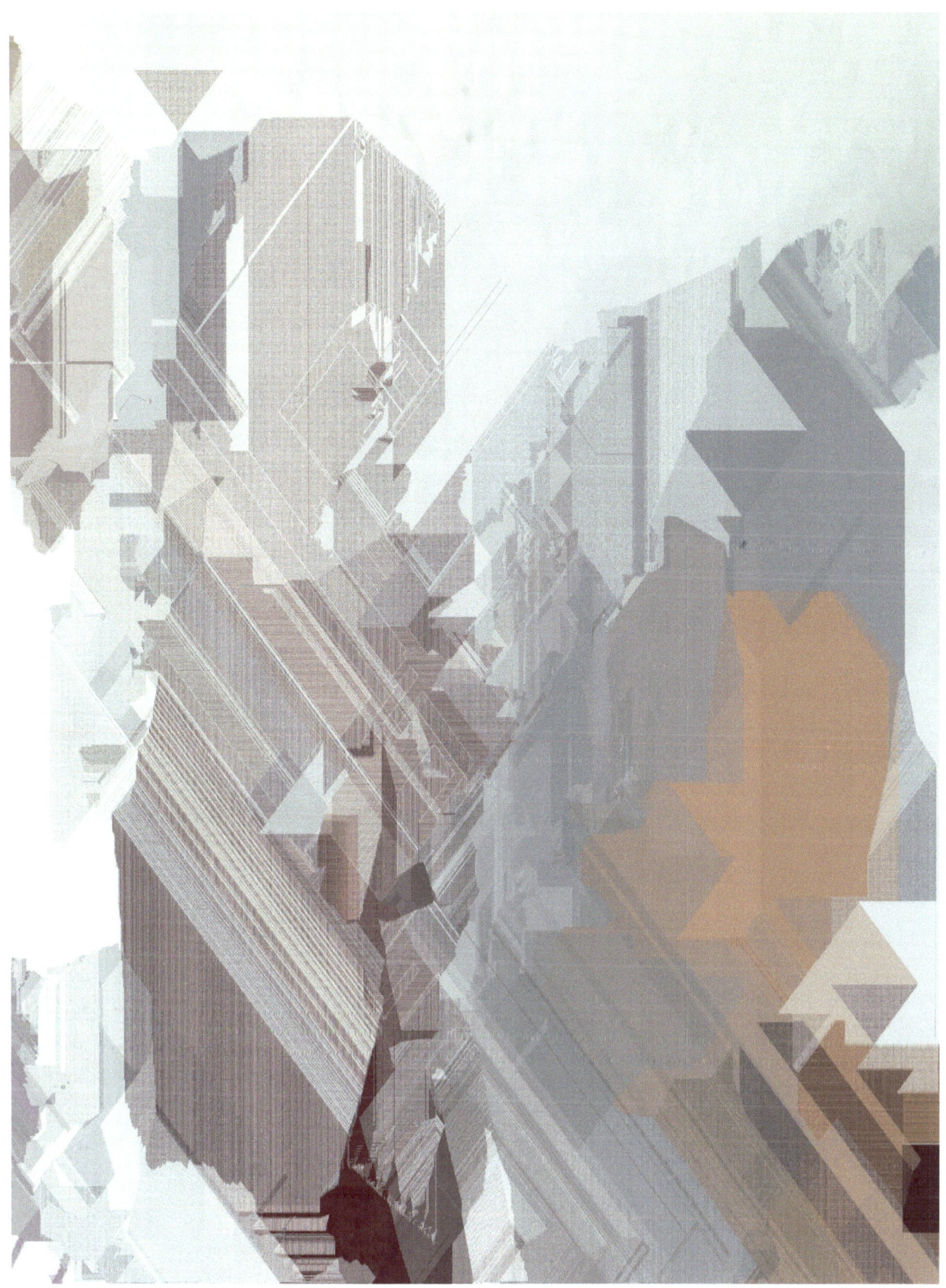

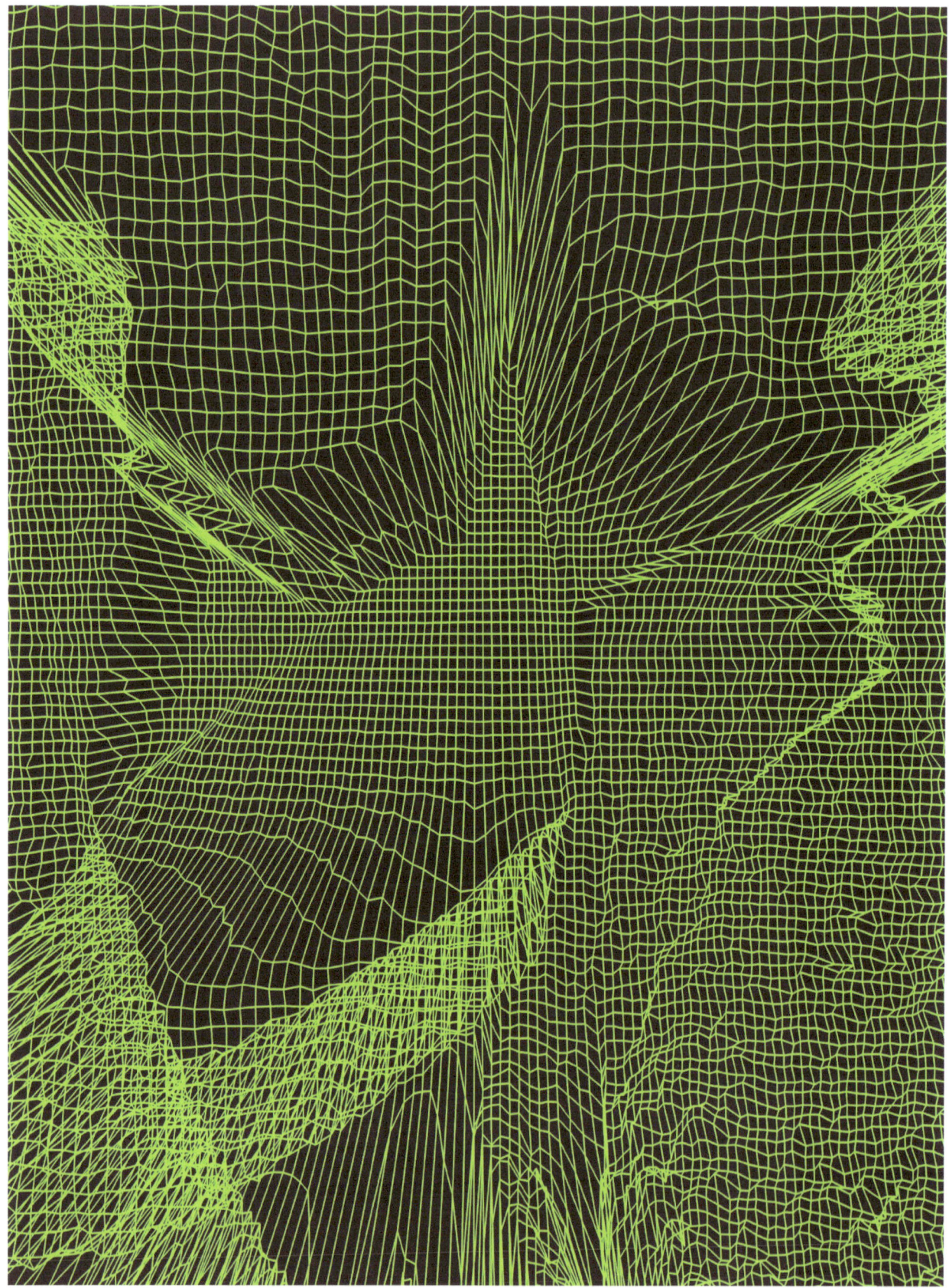

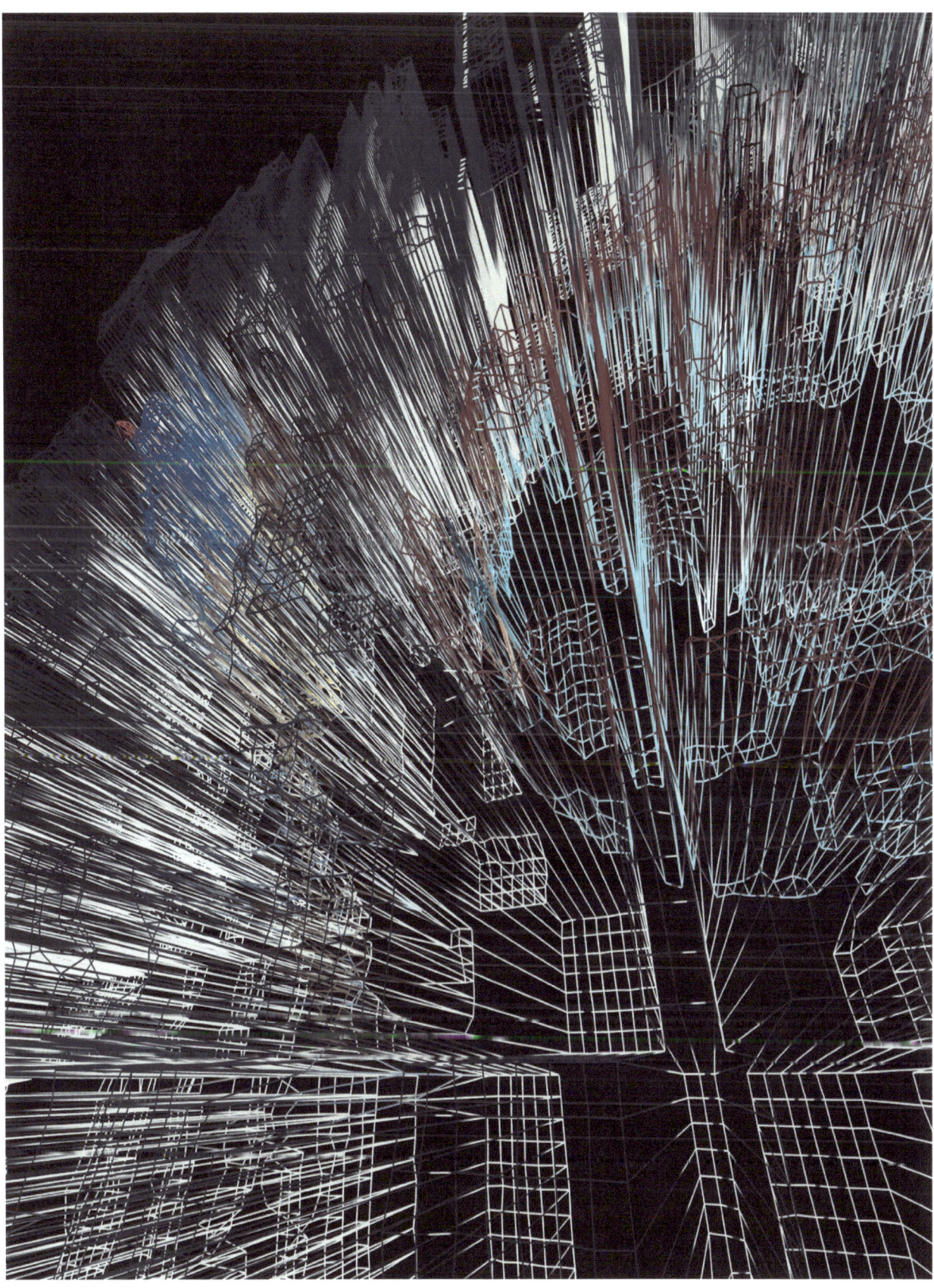

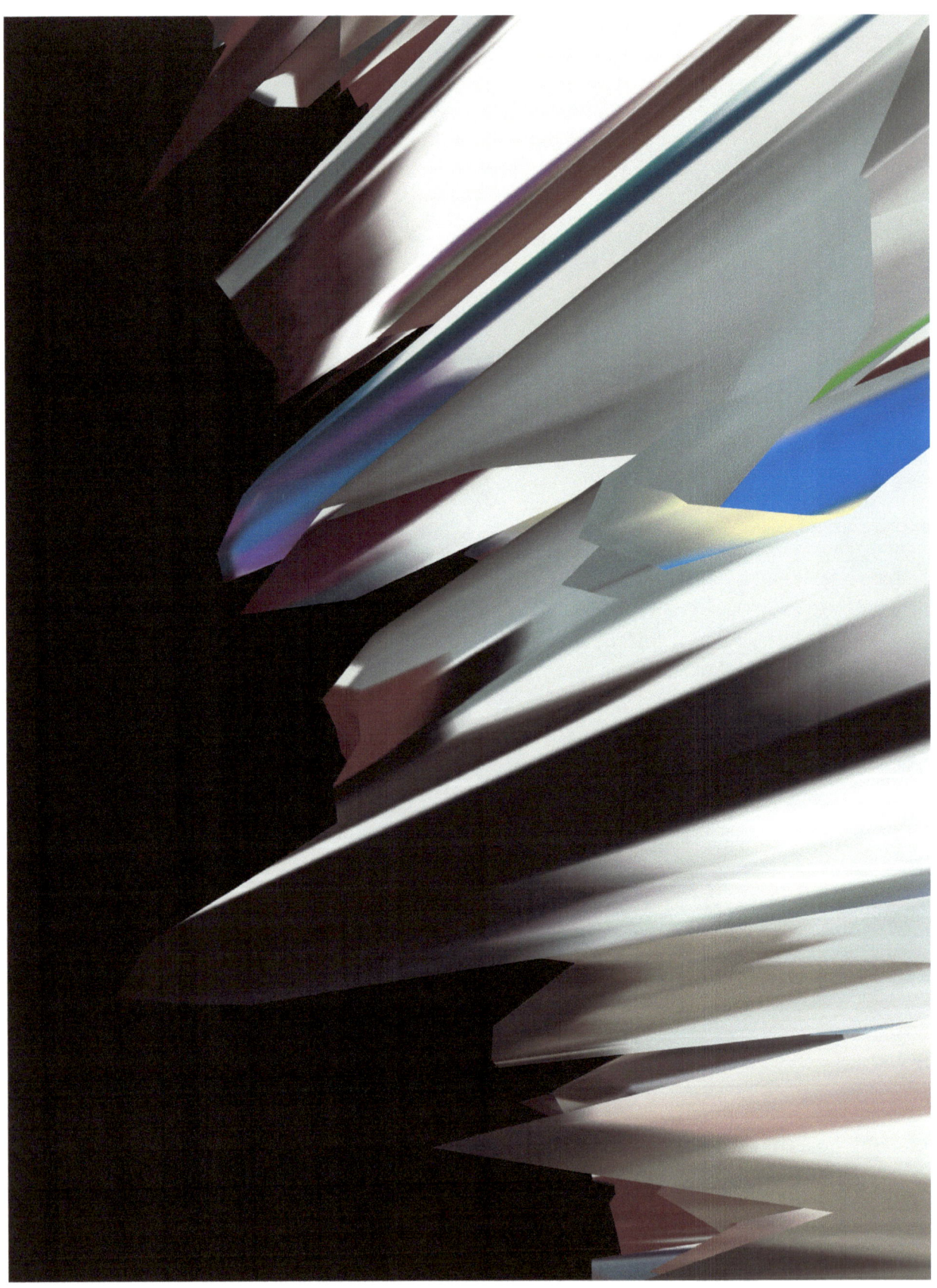

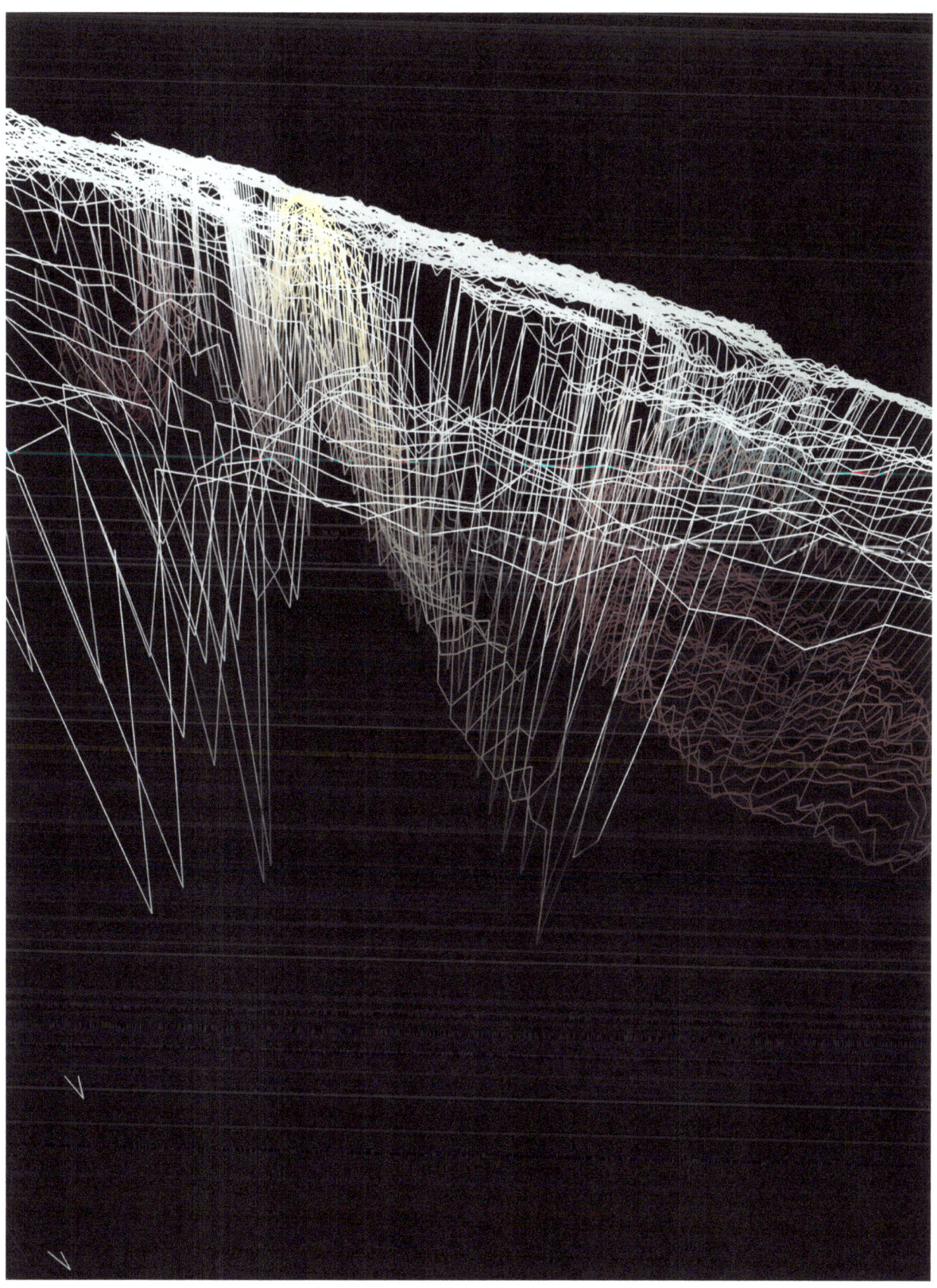

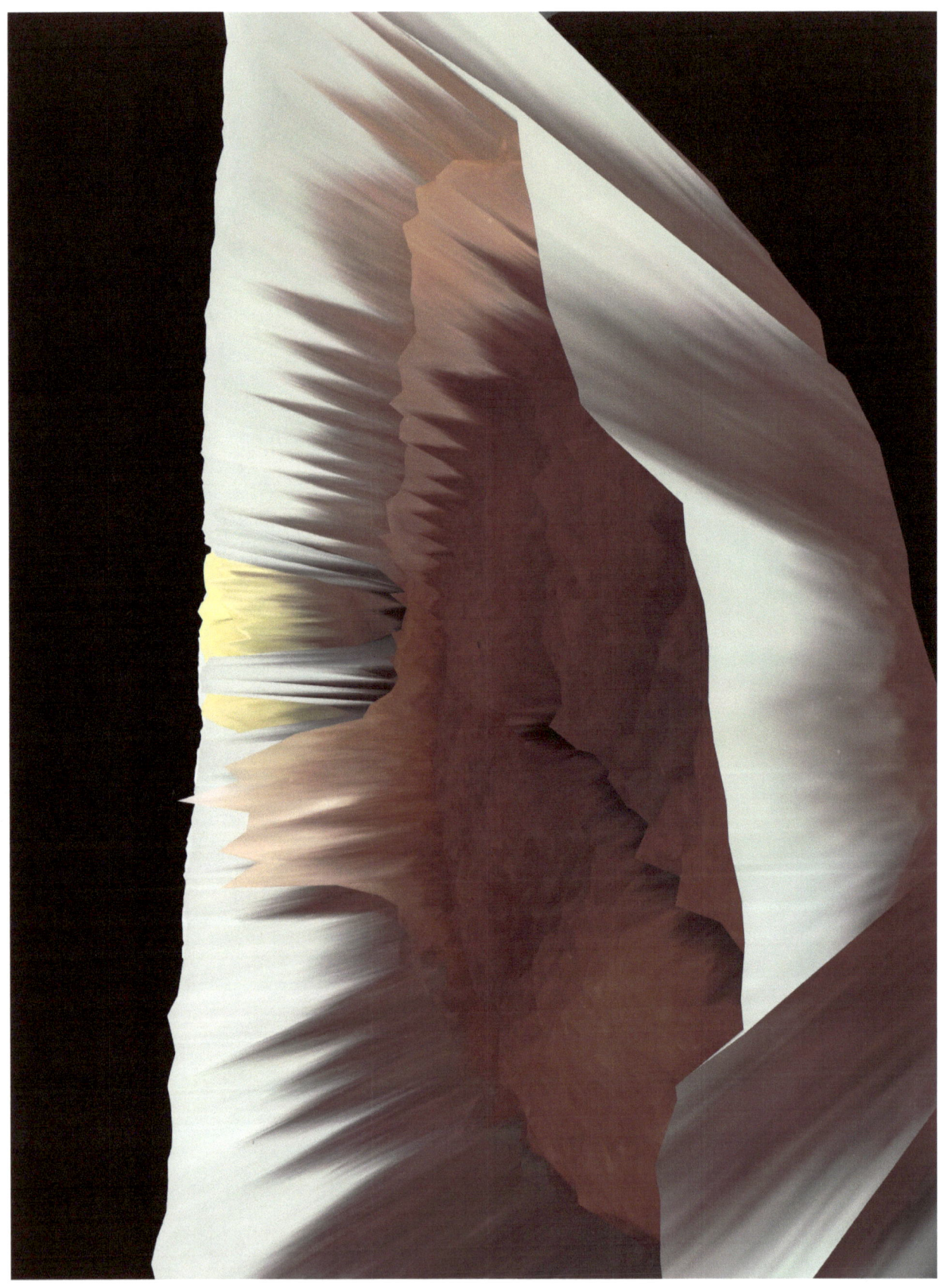

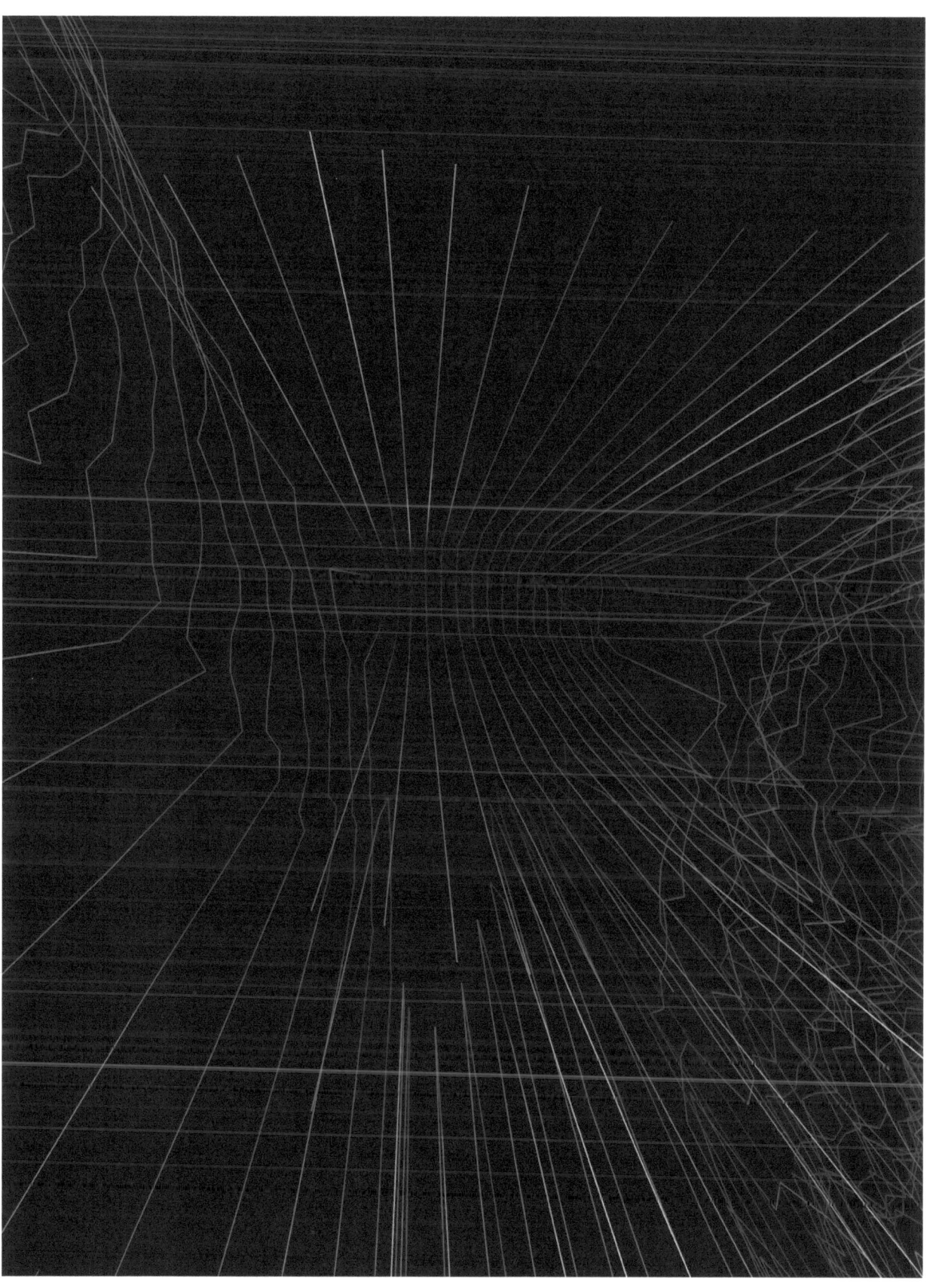

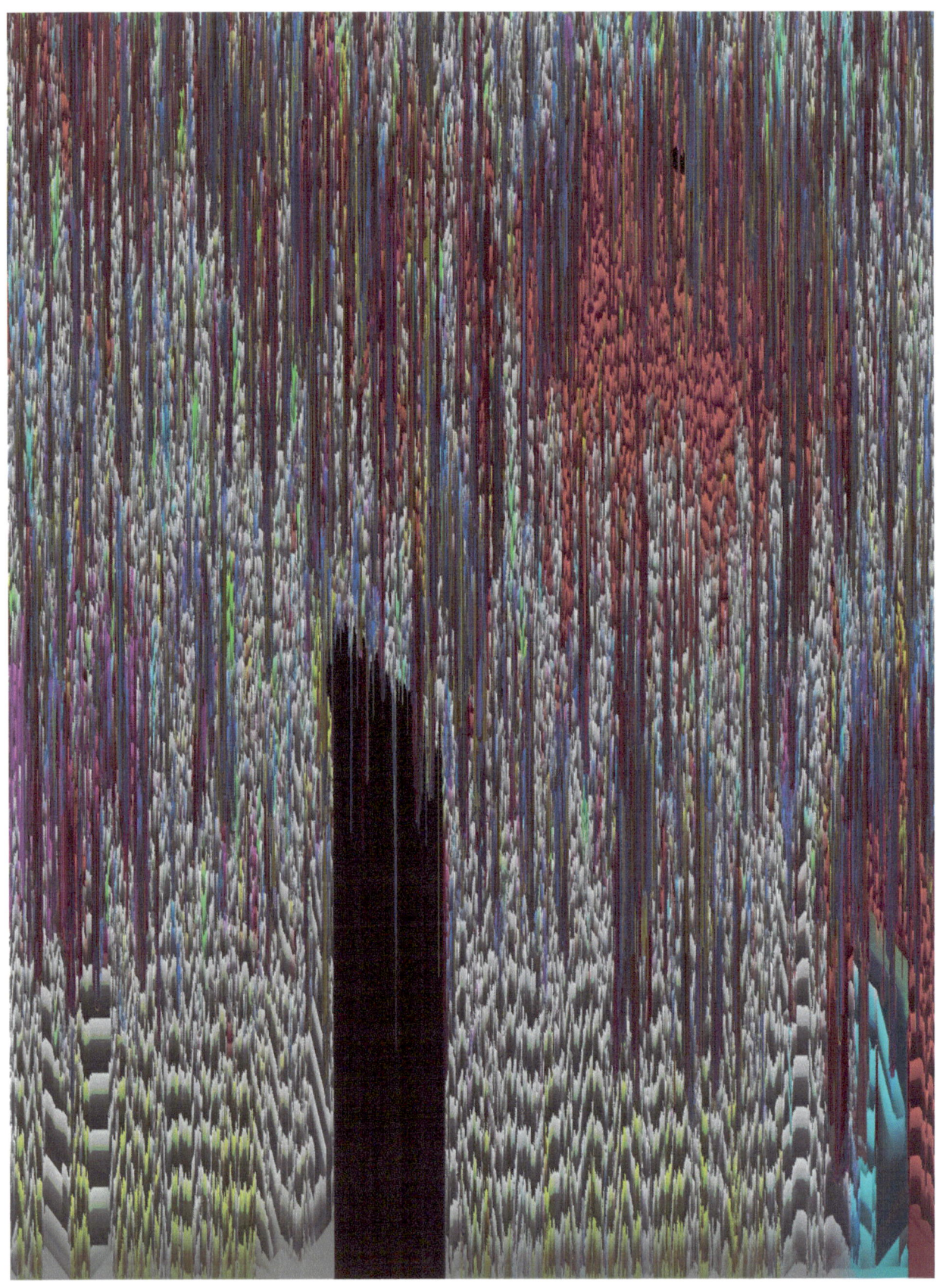

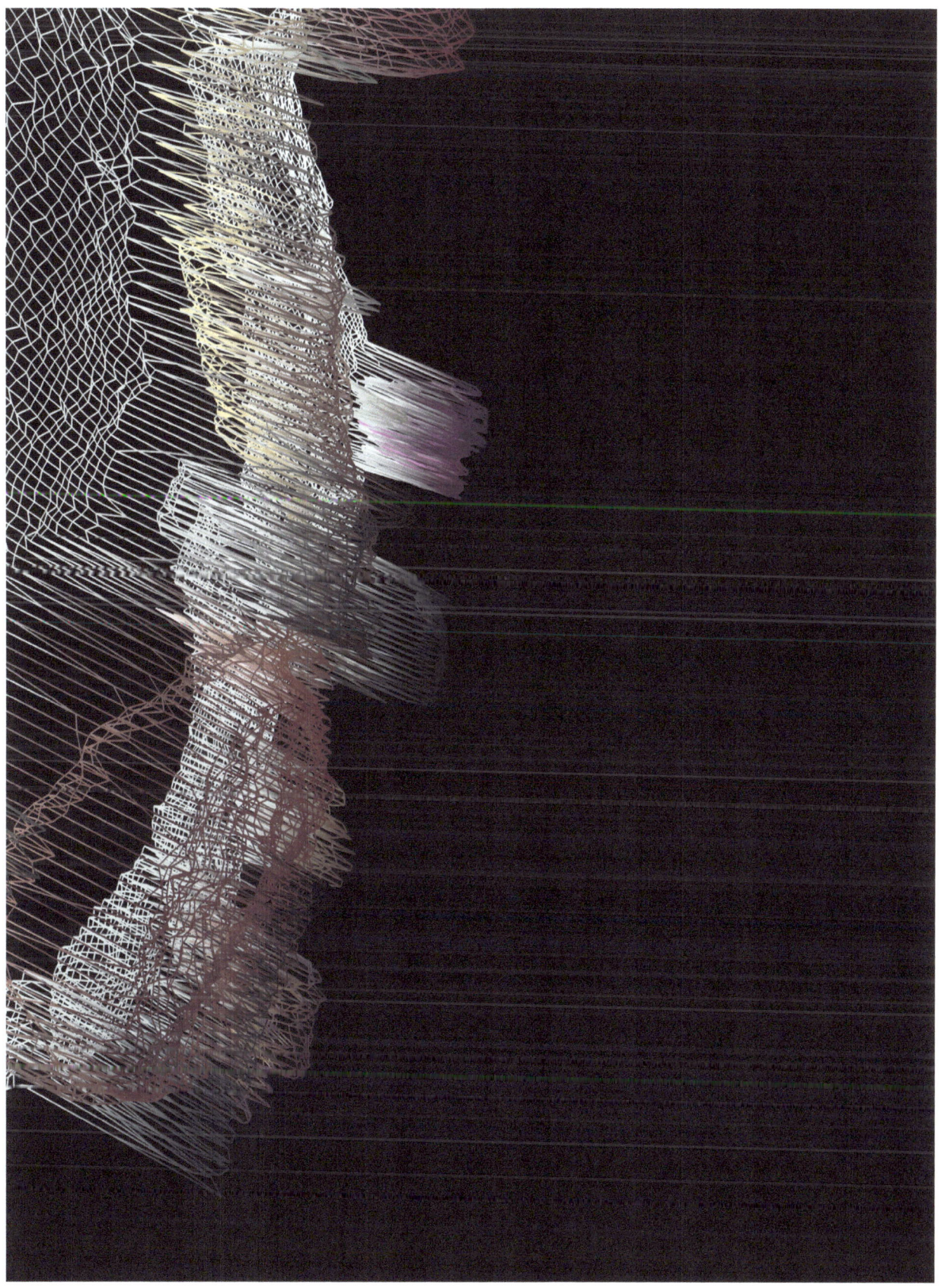

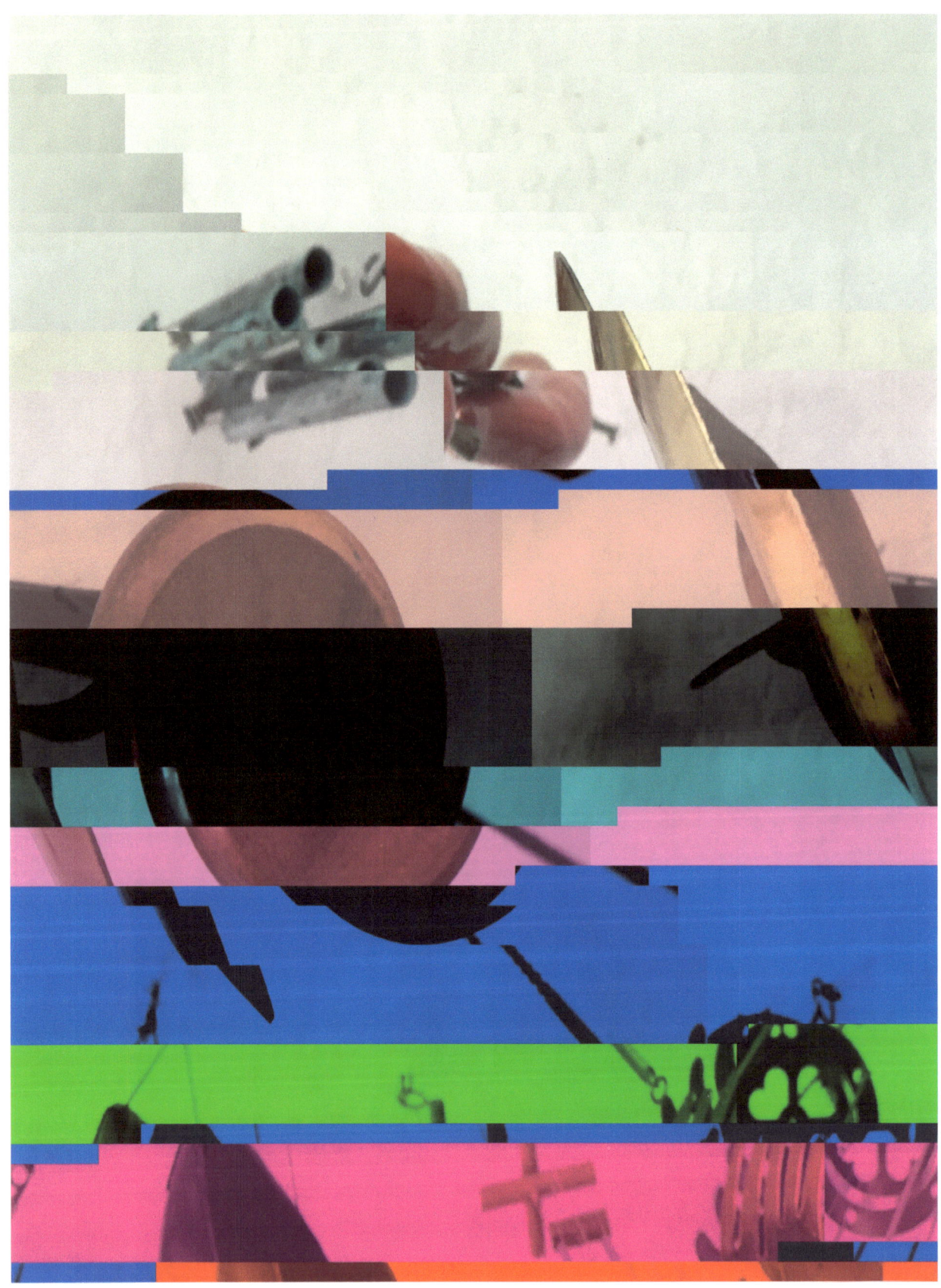

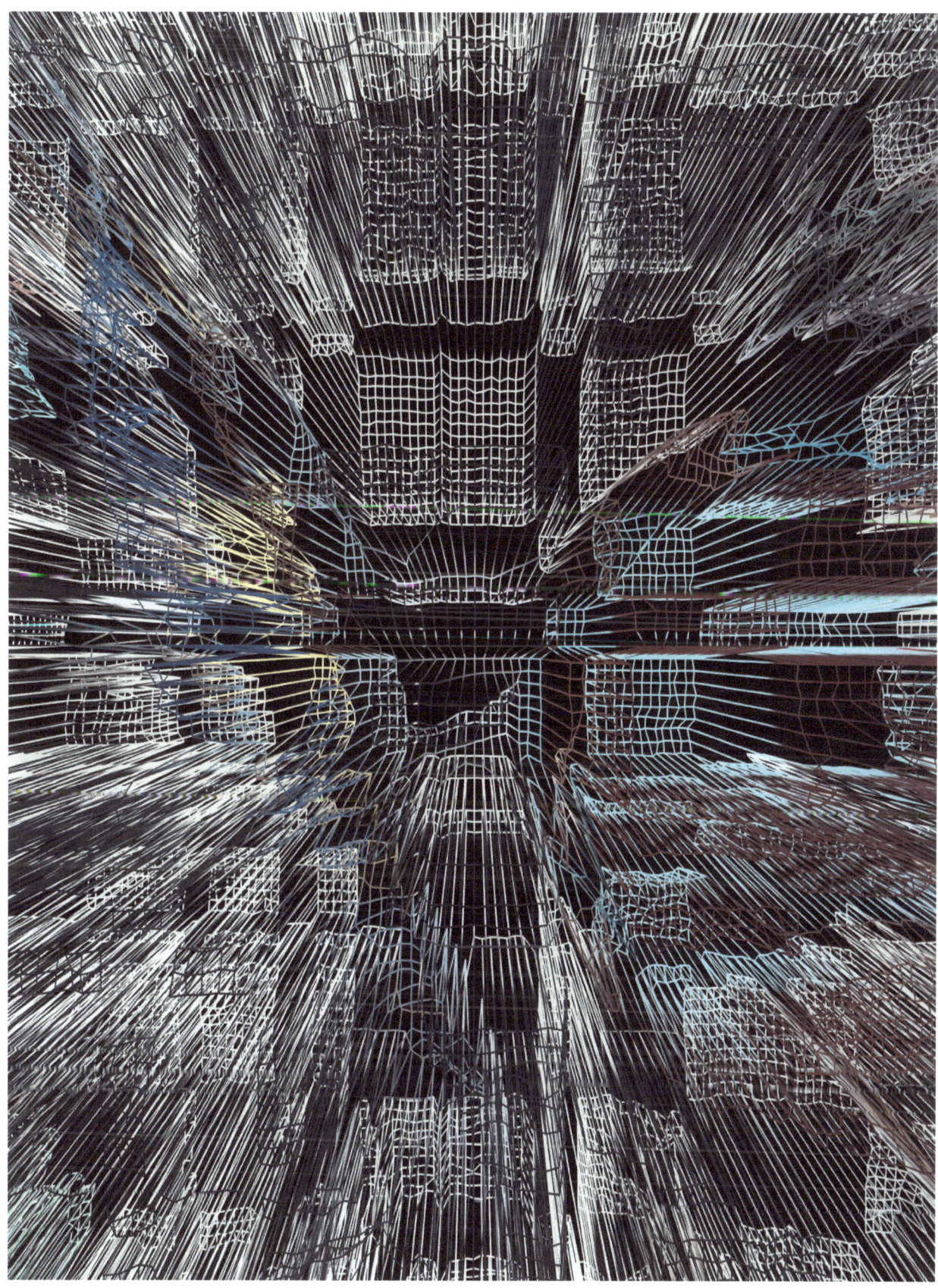

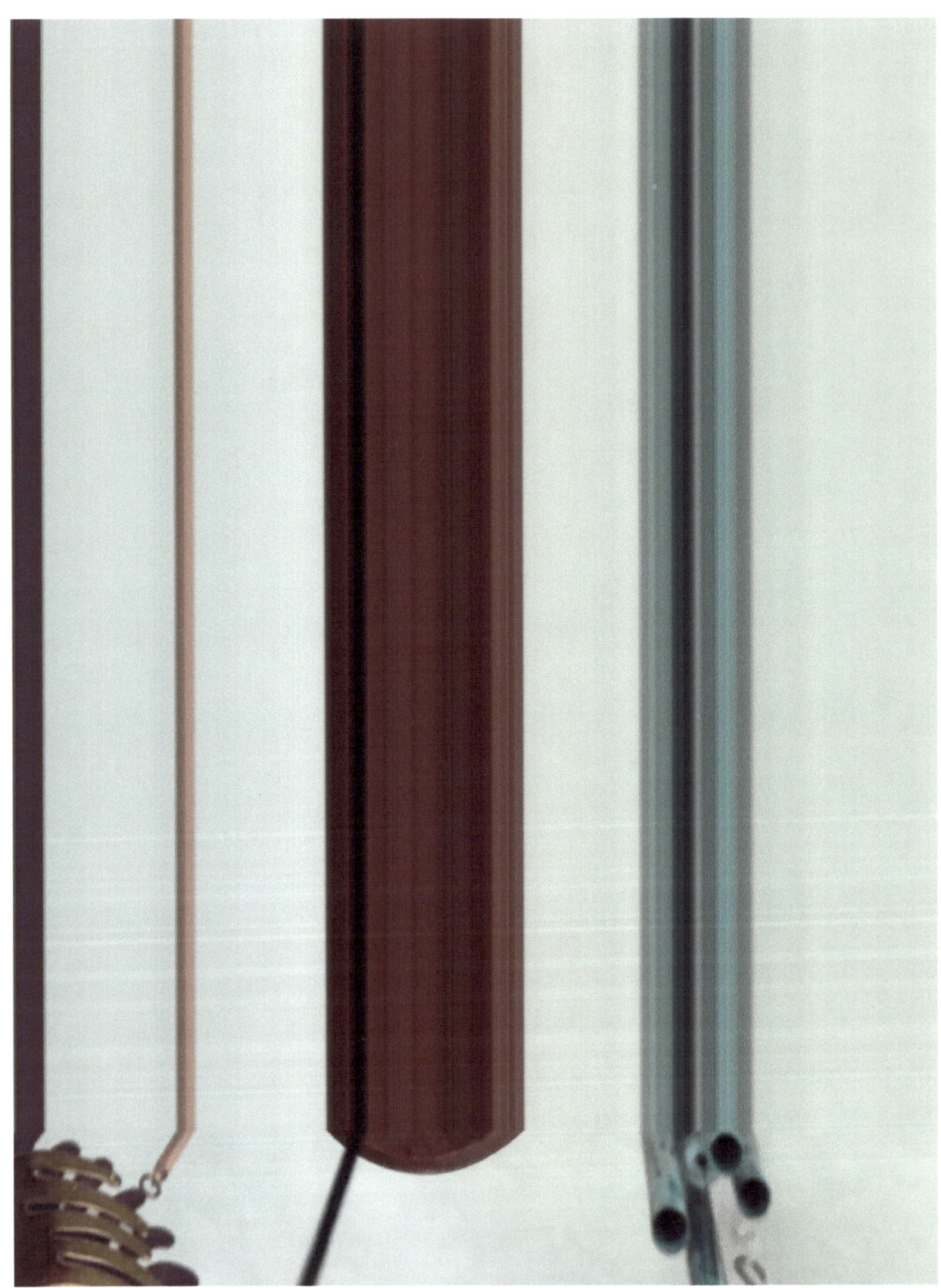

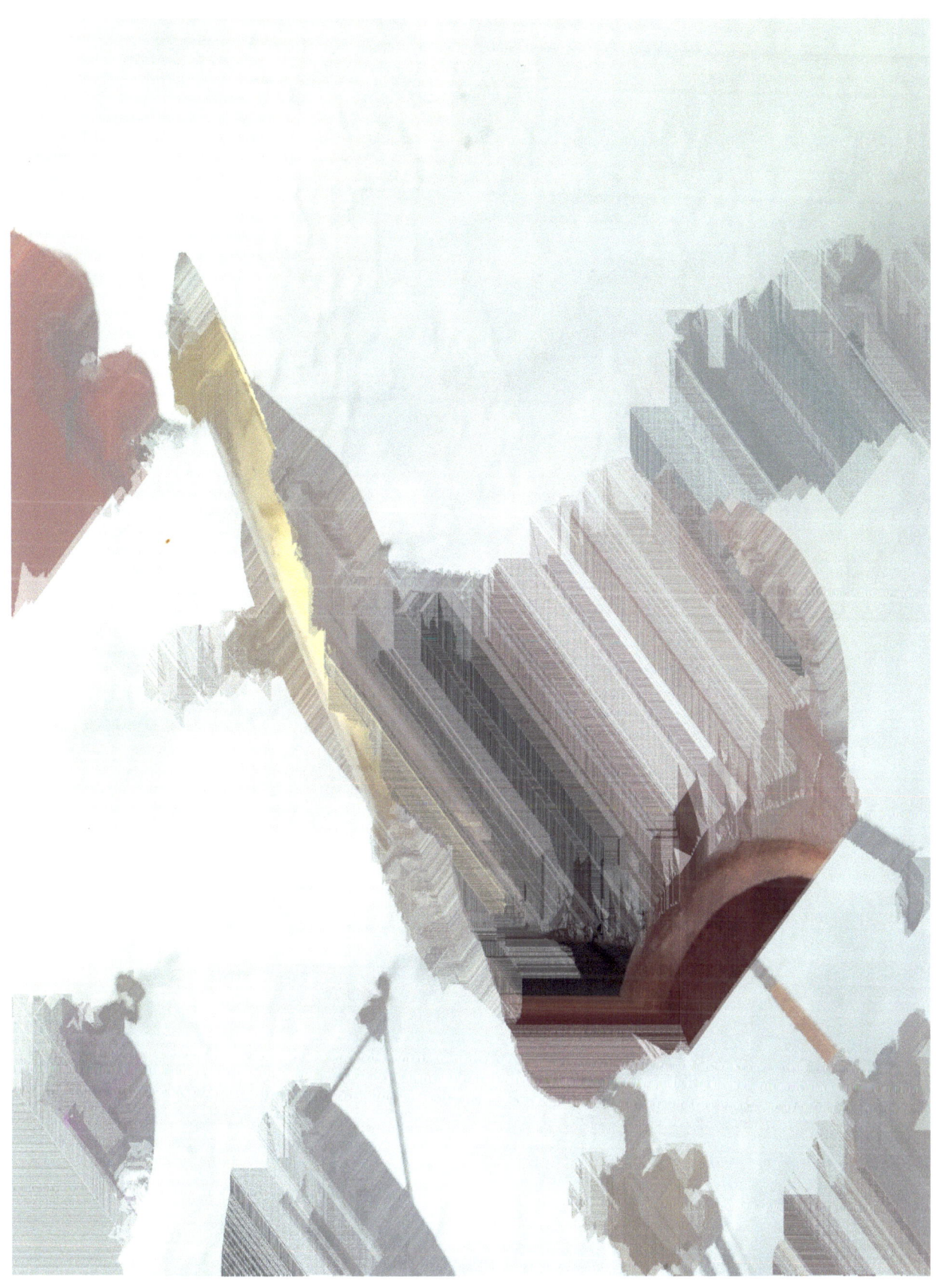

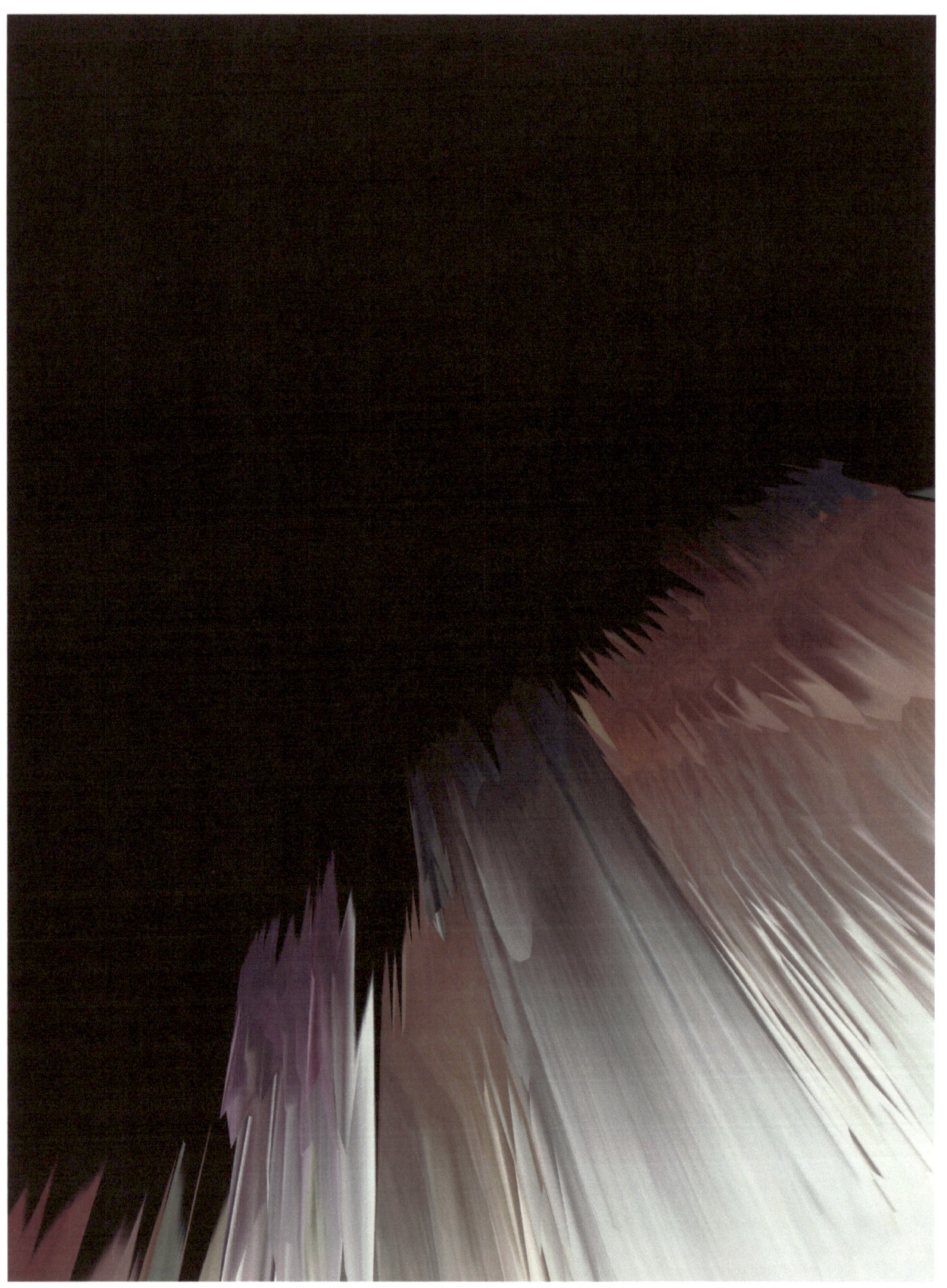

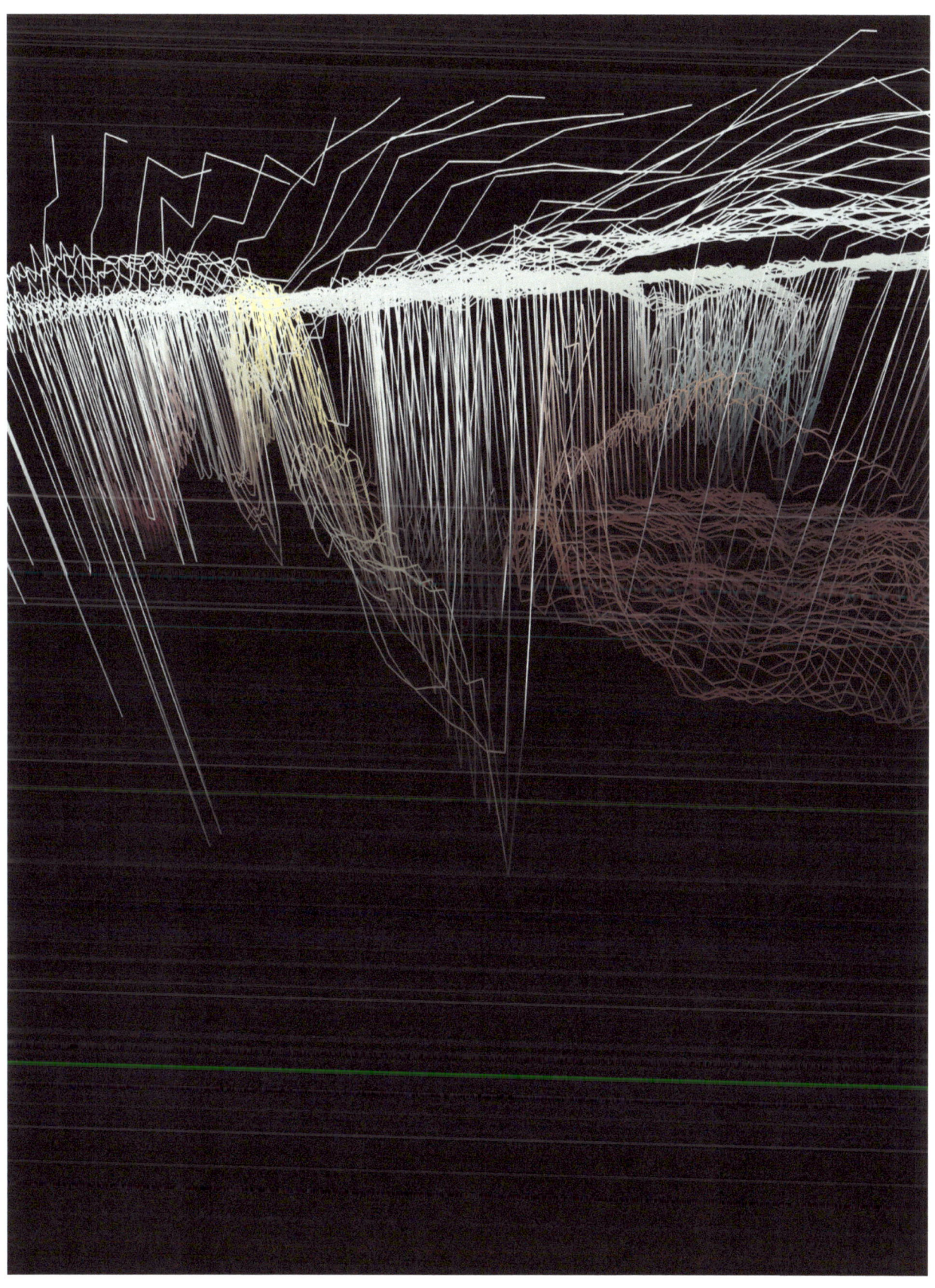

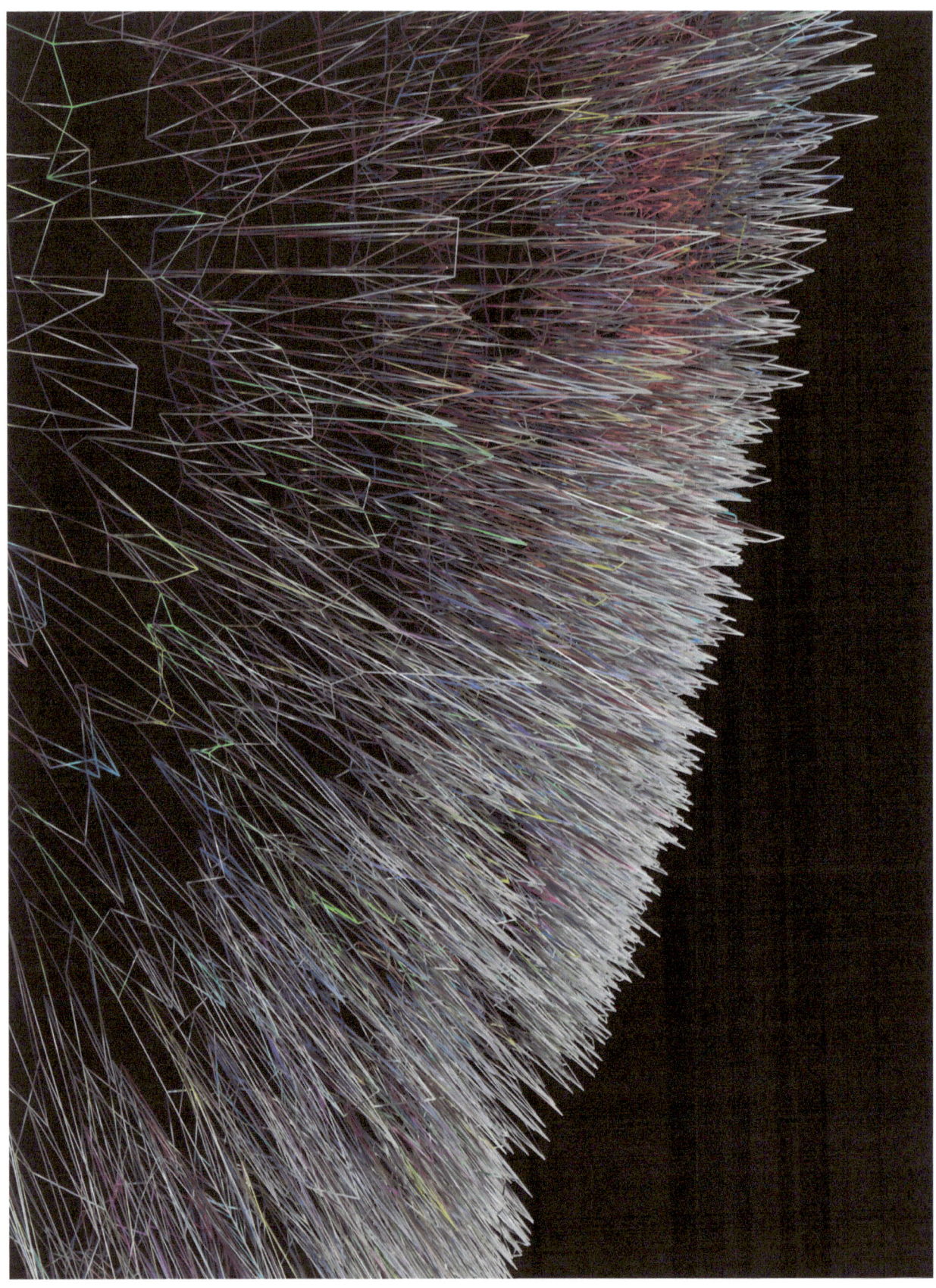

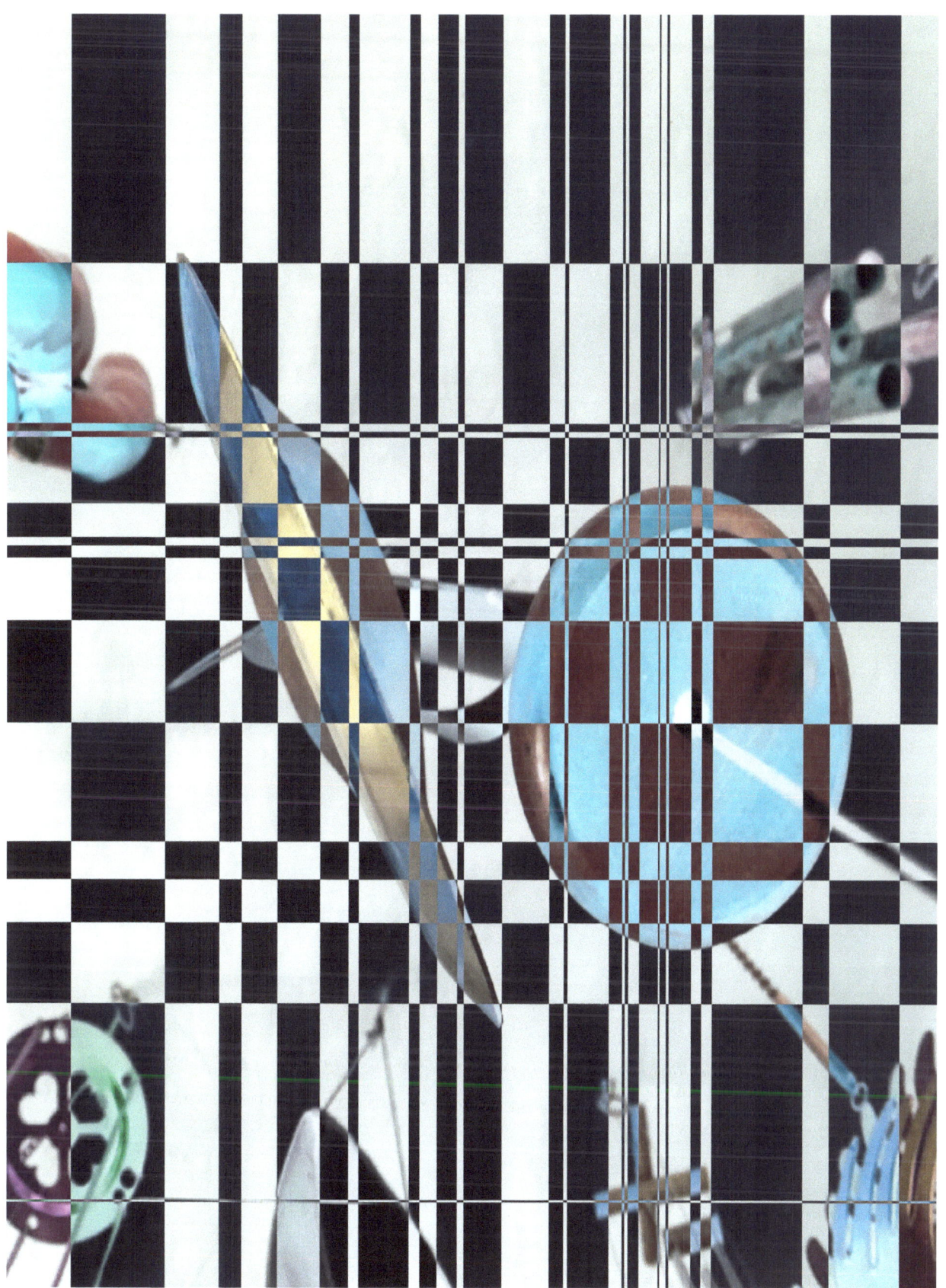

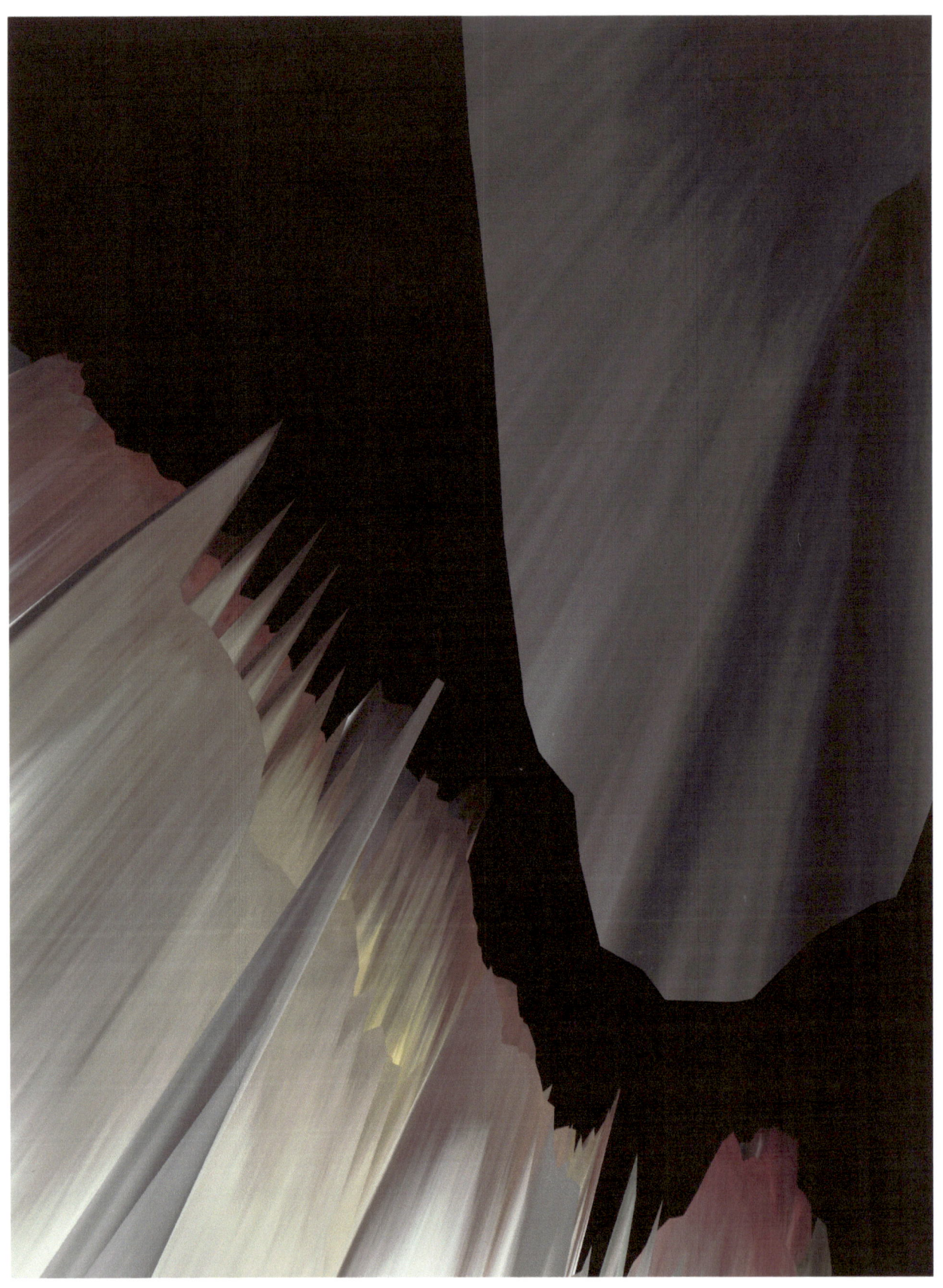

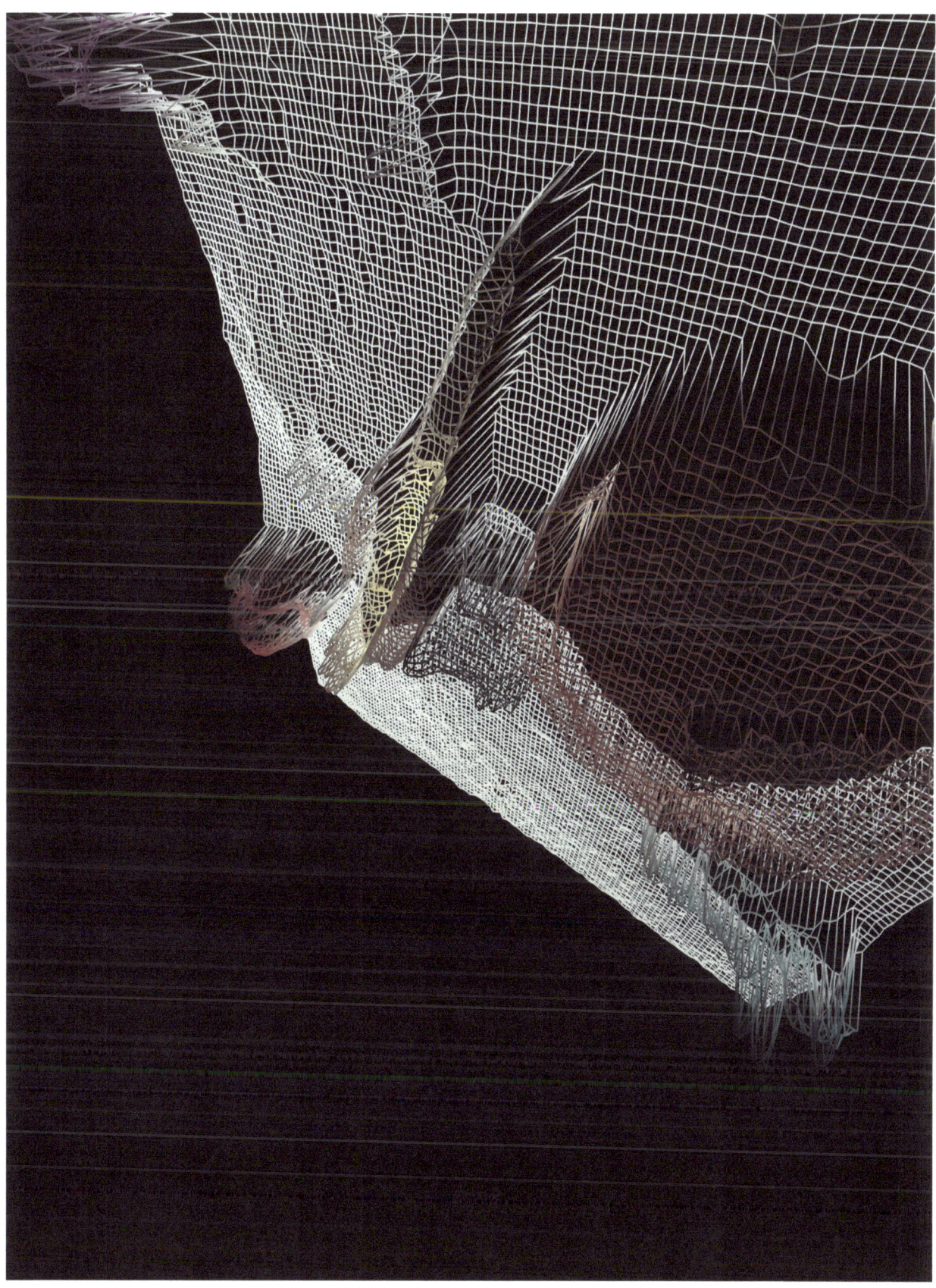

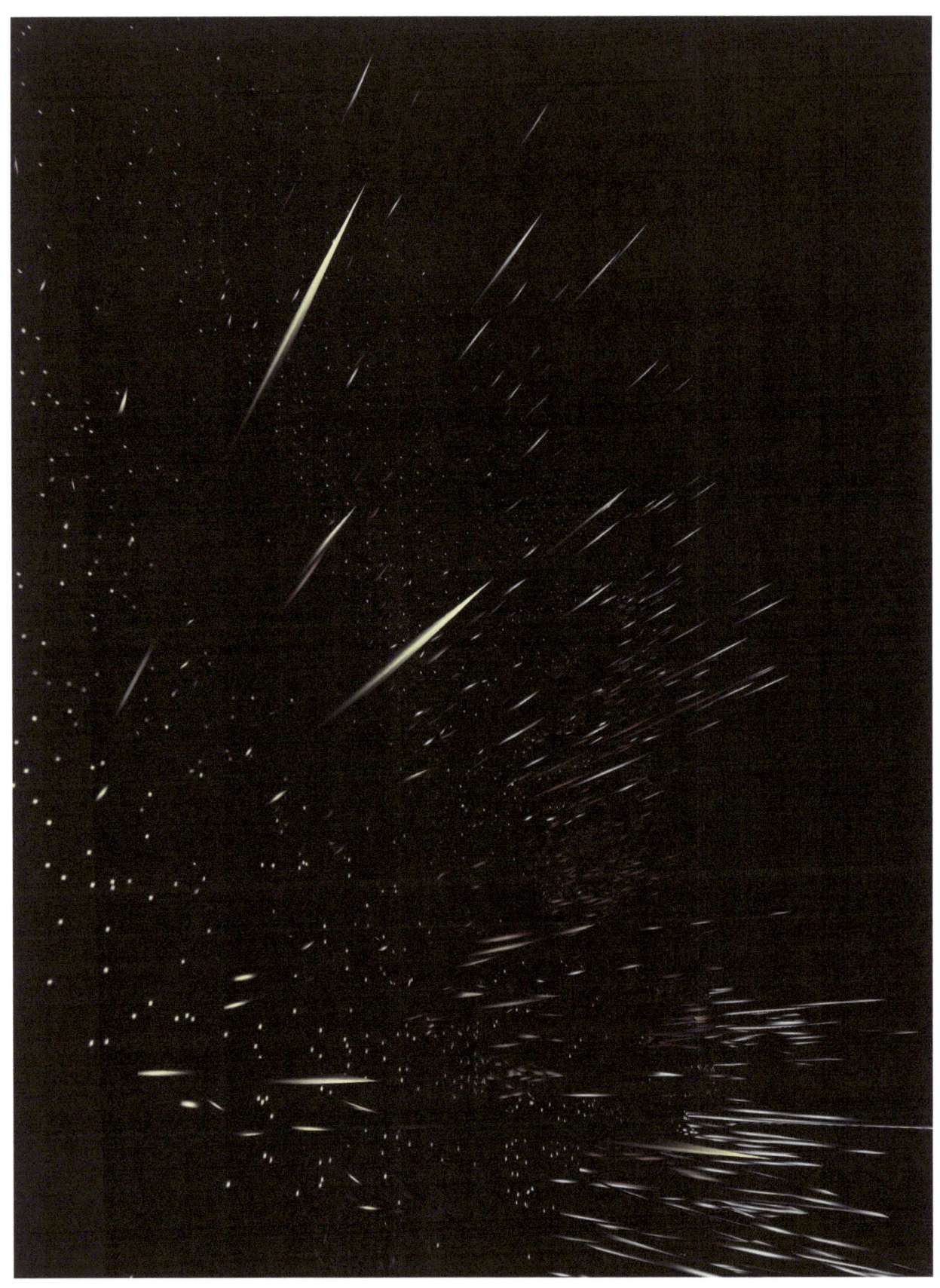

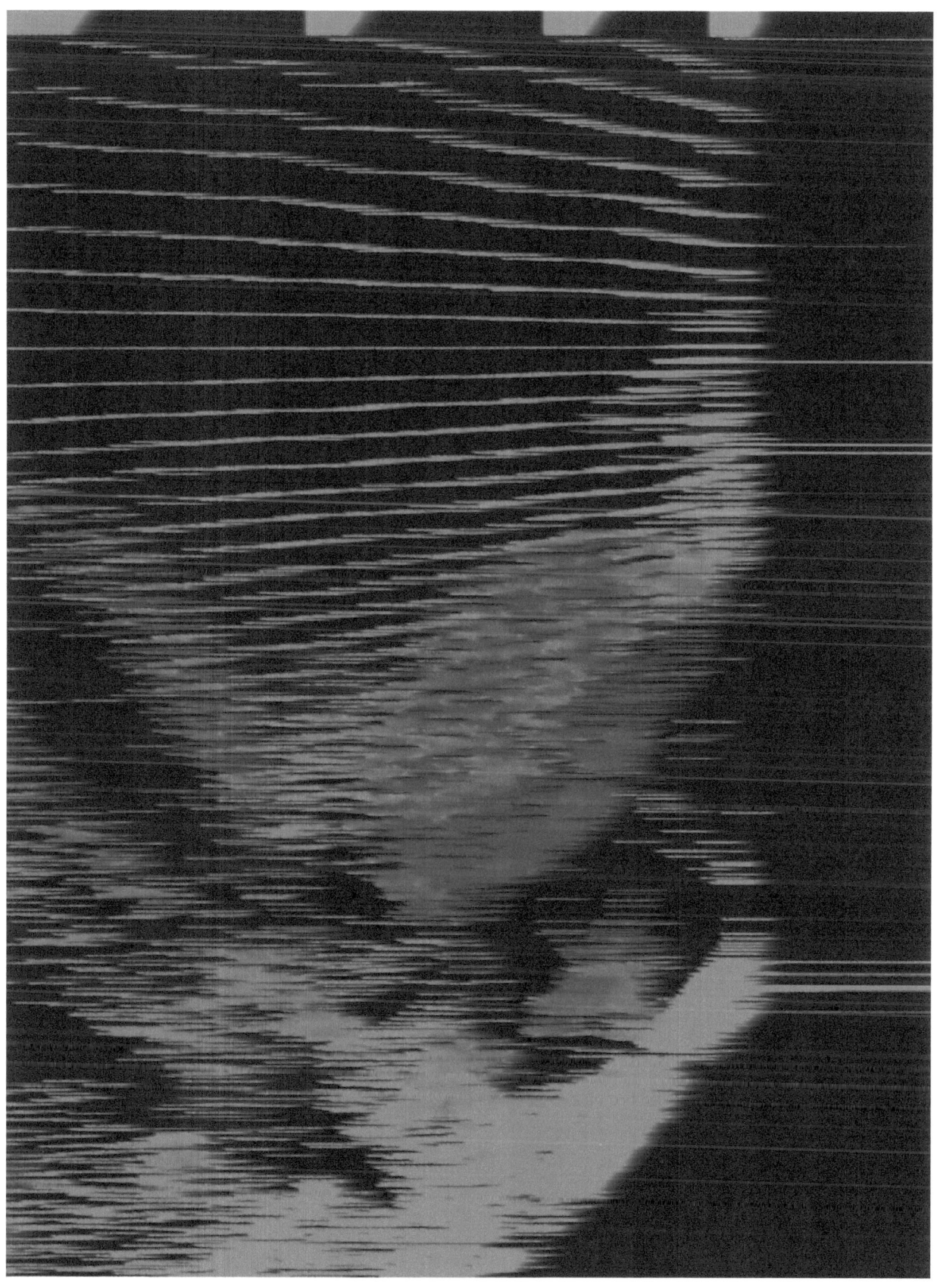

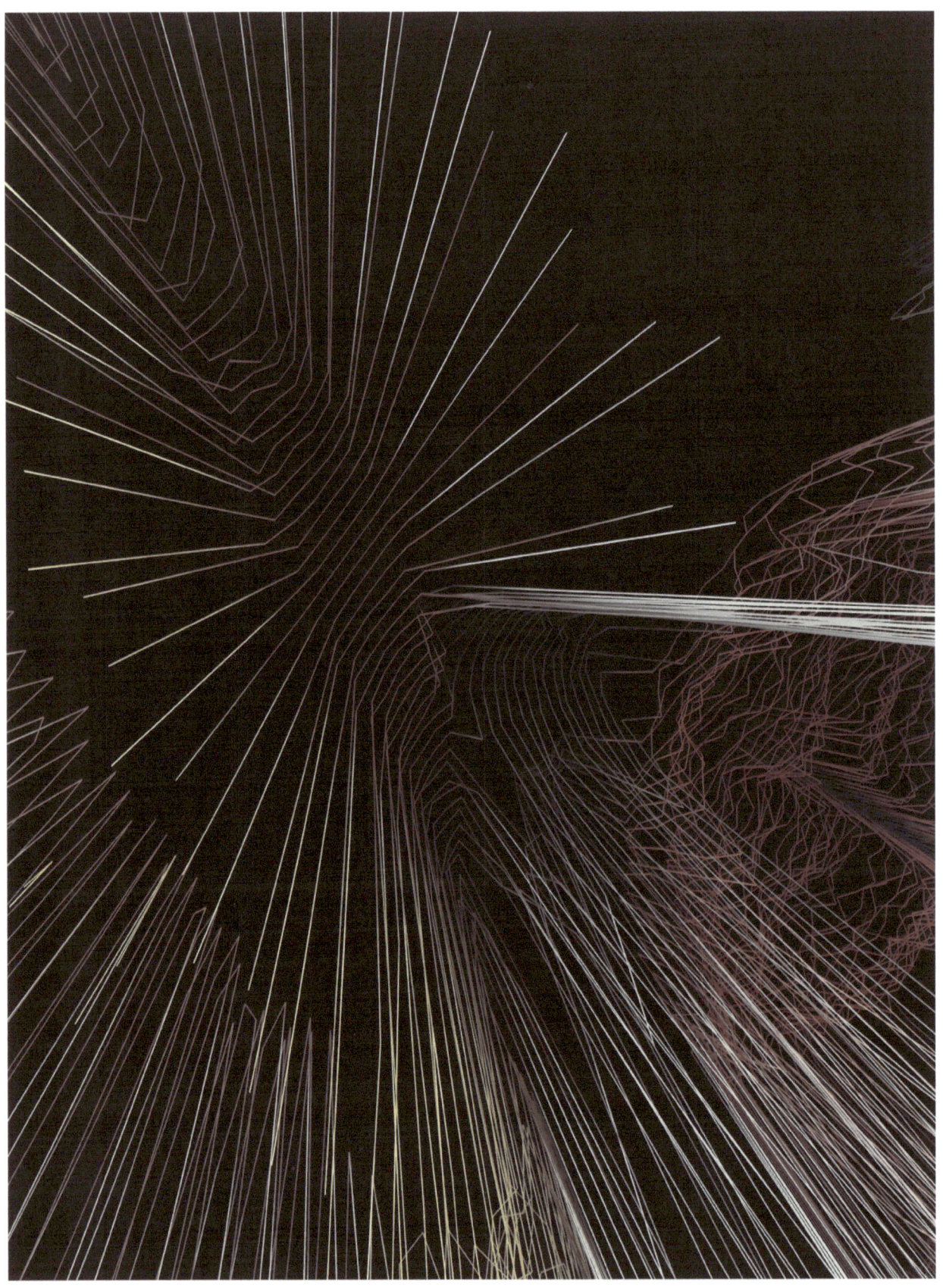

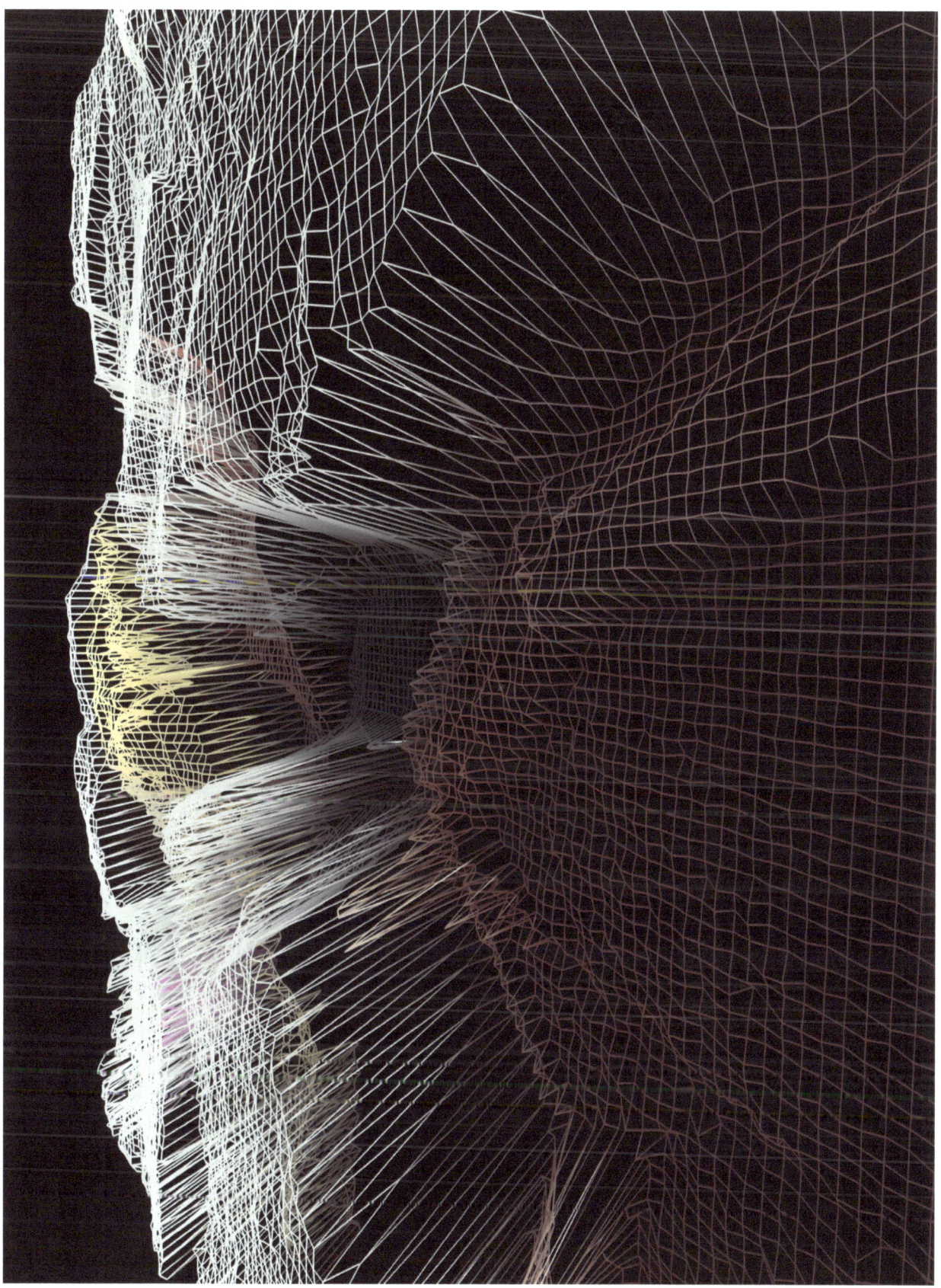

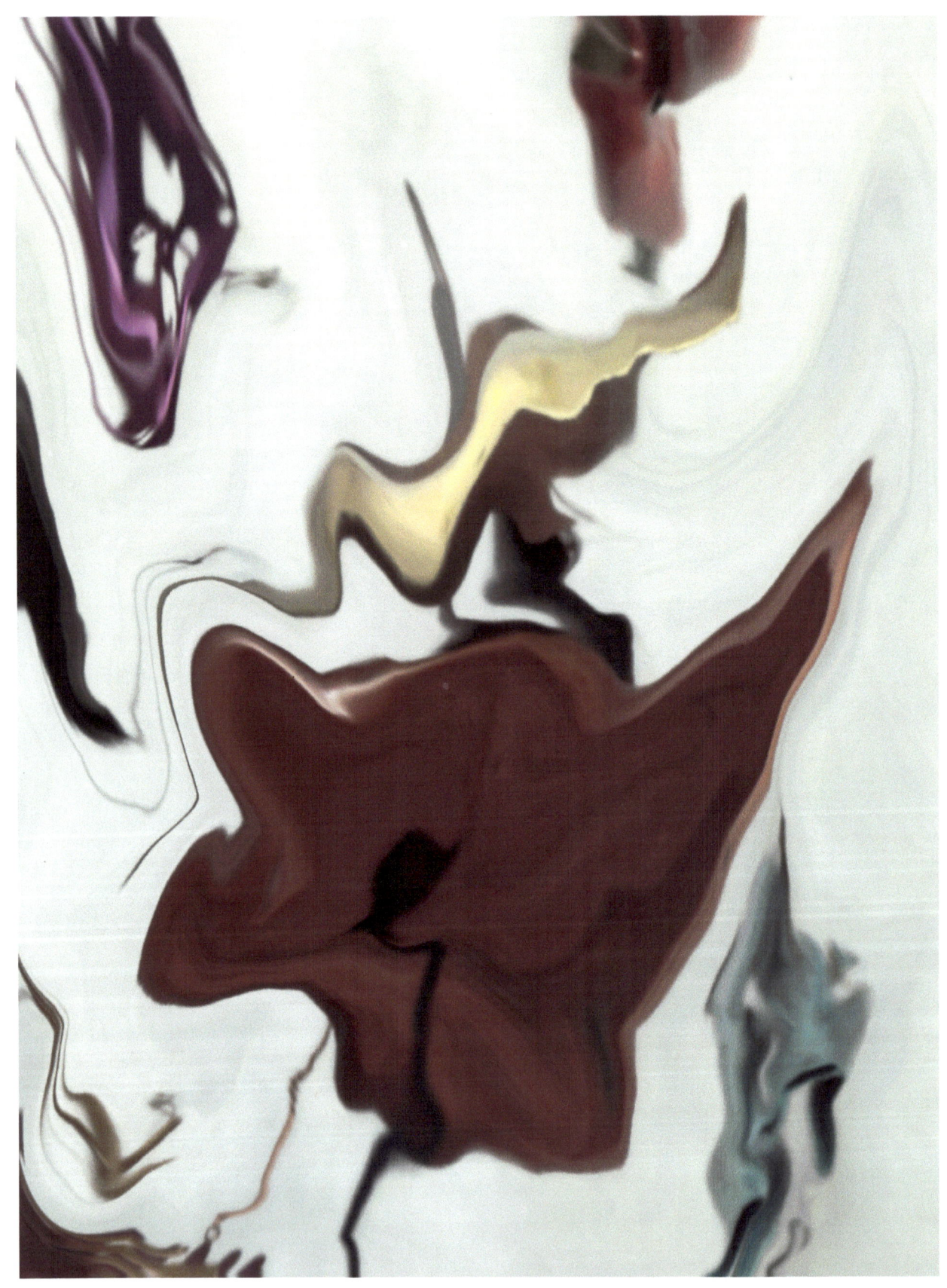